TENDER WHISPERS OF LOVE

SOOTHING WORDS
FOR THE
REAL WORLD

ELLEN RICHARDSON

WestBow
PRESS®
A DIVISION OF THOMAS NELSON
& ZONDERVAN

WestBow Press books may be ordered through booksellers or by contacting:

WestBow Press
A Division of Thomas Nelson & Zondervan
1663 Liberty Drive
Bloomington, IN 47403
www.westbowpress.com
844-714-3454

ISBN: 978-1-6642-0173-6 (sc)
ISBN: 978-1-6642-0172-9 (e)

Library of Congress Control Number: 2020915127

Print information available on the last page.

WestBow Press rev. date: 11/19/2020

CONTENTS

In Appreciation

I would like to thank, first of all, my best friend and Savior, the Lord Jesus Christ, His Spirit, and the Father, for all Their undying, faithful, and mysteriously eternal loving support.

A huge debt of thanks goes out to Teerat Jackree, who worked (and still works) as a volunteer in the computer room of the institution when I was living there in 2002. He was the one who encouraged me to put my writings onto a disk. Without him, there would be no book.

Thanks to my late father, Ronald Joseph Richardson, for all the dear and wonderful memories that I cherish; to my mother for her undying love, someone who has significantly mellowed in her elder years; to Kathleen Sutcliffe and Margot Kidd, who have been real and consistent sources of encouragement over the years; to John Barnes, friend and companion for decades now; to Morris Marshall, who lent his editing eye to the manuscript, and to his wife, Clarice, for all their support; to Dave Painter, another friend for over a decade; and to Lewis Boles, who has been a true and undying supporter and mentor over the years since my paralysis.

Lew himself has no use of his hands or his arms or his legs from a football injury when he was only eighteen. He went on to earn a bachelor's degree in computer science while he lived in the same institution I was in. He stayed there for twenty-nine years; while living there, he was gainfully employed part-time. Then he moved out of that place (which was a feat in itself!) and into an apartment with attendant care; following this, he worked full time for many years from his home, and is presently happily married and retired. He has been an inspiration to me as he continues in his quest to be an advocate for all those with a spinal cord injury.

I'd also like to thank my dear mother and sister, in particular, who helped me create a home for myself, post-injury.

I also extend my deep and heartfelt gratitude again to my sister and my lawyer, David McGhee, for all their work on the lawsuit.

Introduction

"Life can be so good, and life can be so hard," sings recording artist Kathy Troccoli. We can be whistling a tune as we go along, when suddenly, life takes a dramatic turn, and we plunge headlong into the depths. We can one day be enjoying the very best life has to offer and the following day plummet into deep despair.

The times we live in are perilous, to say the least. As I'm writing, the world is in the throes of a pandemic, coronavirus or COVID-19. To date, there have been over a million deaths world-wide because of it. If that's not enough, other troubles can come at us from seemingly nowhere—other serious health problems, family issues, separation, divorce, accidents, including car wrecks— and when we least expect them, deep, horrific troubles. It's also true that we all travel on a narrow road, a path full of pitfalls and potholes.

Where do we turn, someone might ask? What do we do? Do we turn to each other? Of course, we can. We all need each other, after all. That said, no one person can possibly meet all our needs. No one can be there for us twenty-four/seven. And when they are there for us, do they say just what we need to hear? And when they say what we need to hear, there's no guarantee that they will be available for us the next time we need them. "Oh, dear," someone then might say, "so where *do* we turn?"

When you get right down to it, we are all on an individual, unique, and therefore sometimes lonely journey. No two persons have the same life, not even identical twins. Life can throw curveballs at us, and we can find ourselves walking through deserts of time when we are faced with God—and God only. Someone once said, "When God is all you have, you realize He is all you need."

We can turn to God, but is He *really* enough? Through no fault of my own, I have gone through periods when I did not have one close friend or relative. Oh, I had friends but no one following me closely. During those times, I dug into Jesus and my journaling with Him. He guided me and comforted me in a dialogue, as only He could. Realizing that He knows me better than I know myself, I thought, *Who better to go to?*

Living with two major disabilities, I'm here to say that God is enough. Jesus is enough. Recall that the very first of the Ten Commandments is to have "no other gods before me" (Exodus 20:3; Deuteronomy 5:7). This is teaching that is often overlooked. As prolific author and speaker Joyce Meyer says, so many pick up the phone when they should be going to the throne. God is a loving God, for sure, but He is also "a jealous God"—this phrase is repeated in scripture many times for emphasis. He yearns for spiritual intimacy with all his followers. He brings trials our way to help foster this.

The great apostle Paul wrote,

> We do not want you to be uninformed, brothers and sisters, about the troubles we experienced in the province of Asia. We were under great pressure, far beyond our ability to endure, so that we despaired of life itself. Indeed, we felt we had received the sentence of death. (2 Corinthians 1:8–9a)

Maybe you don't feel like this presently and find it difficult to relate to at the moment, but wait. You never know what is around the corner. I never planned to live my life in a wheelchair, but here I sit! In hindsight, of course, I'm so grateful to be alive, but still, I wouldn't have chosen this. We need to prepare for the unknown future to fortify us, should such feelings as the ones Paul lists here arise. As well, if Paul, the author of so many of the books in the

New Testament, felt like this, how much more are *we* prone to feeling like that? What happens when we despair of life itself? Is God really enough, even then?

I was raised an atheist, but in the summer of 1987, when I was in my twenties, while deeply depressed, so many monarch butterflies flew into my line of vision that I could not help but conclude that Someone was trying to get my attention. Soon thereafter, a friend, who didn't know about the butterflies, invited me to her church. With my newfound belief in the existence of God, when the faithful pastor there gave an altar call, I received the forgiveness of Jesus for my sins, making him Lord of my life. And my life has never been the same since.

A year prior to my accepting Christ, I was also diagnosed with a biochemical disease of the brain called depression, or major depressive disorder. This condition has no known cure but is treatable with medication. Despite my conversion, I spent many years coming to grips with my need for the meds, but when I did, my disease went into remission, so much so that I was able to complete a bachelor of religious education (BRE) degree and a master of divinity (MDiv) in counseling, graduating in 1998.

This book has a major premise: that just as we had no say in how we came into the world, we are to have no say in how we leave the world; that all suffering has meaning in the eternal realm. In other words, suicide is not an option, whether by one's own hands or physician-assisted. I learned that the hard way.

Sadly, because of the biochemical condition in my brain, I tried to end my life on three separate occasions, all serious attempts. In fact, with one of my attempts in 2001, my family filed a lawsuit shortly after the event. The lawsuit itself took twelve years, but I'm happy to say that we won. It claimed certain psychiatrists were responsible for a jump from a bridge known for it's lethality, a most desperate act that left me without the abilities to walk or to stand. While I take full responsibility for what I did, if not for the inaction of a number of specialists, I would not be in a chair today.

I went from suicidal despair immediately post-injury to, three and a half years later, being nicknamed "Ellen of Joy" by a friend.

Given time and a relationship with Christ, there is no telling what He can accomplish in you.

The line that follows the quoted scripture, above, reads as follows: "But this happened that we might not rely on ourselves but on God, who raises the dead" (2 Corinthians 1:9b). Jesus has enough power for all of us, no matter what we face!

I say it again: God is enough. Jesus is enough. If you still have doubts, recall the first verse of the most-famous Twenty-Third Psalm (NKJV): "The Lord is my Shepherd. I shall not want" as well as, "And my God shall supply all your need according to His riches in glory by Christ Jesus" (Philippians 4:19 NKJV).

Living in this world, however, can be wearying. Is life just so complicated, so complex, and just plain exhausting that you wonder when it'll ever end? Is *How Far Is Heaven?* by Salvador your song?

In this book, I offer the comfort I have received (2 Corinthians 1:3–5) from Jesus over the years. As you walk along your narrow path, I pray these words can help strengthen, fortify, and even delight you at times.

Within these pages, we will walk together to discover just how we can not only survive but thrive, even in and through deep pain, as we learn to surrender it fully to Jesus. With His help, you too can learn to press on victoriously, even in the midst of the most agonizing and relentless of circumstances.

This book has a companion, *Tender Whispers of Love: Poetry*, which I also drafted while living in the institution for my paraplegia.

Both books are geared for the war-weary and heaven-bent.

CHAPTER ONE

ALAS, LIFE IS DIFFICULT

We hope and pray that life will go our way, but there is no escaping the fact that it is sometimes full of trouble. Psychiatrist M. Scott Peck begins his best-selling book, *The Road Less Traveled*, with the three powerful words: "Life is difficult." The truth is, children can taunt and harass their siblings and classmates. Adults can gossip and tear strips off each other with bitter arguments and harsh words they may later regret. We can find ourselves in such painful circumstances that we wonder where love is in the world at all.

A line from the movie *The Princess Bride* says that life is pain, and anyone telling you any different "is trying to sell you something." Another challenging reality. The movie goes further and even speaks in an offhanded way of "the cliffs of insanity." You don't have to live in the adult world too long before you come to know these.

Someone might ask, "Why do you speak of all this tough, heavy stuff? I've got enough heavy stuff in my own life." I want to help you see that it is precisely the heavy stuff that draws us closer to God, and builds our faith and character, which is the only thing we will take with us when we die (according to Joni Eareckson Tada, artist, prolific writer, radio personality, ministry founder, and quadriplegic). Whether we like to think of it or not, death—another challenging reality—is a certainty. We will all face it at one time or another. Are you ready? All life is but a preparation for us to make that final passage from this life into the next.

Understandably, we can seek to escape the difficult truths of life in various ways, some of which are healthy; others that are not. We can seek diversion in books, in movies, in fellowship with each other or we can look for solace in illegal drugs, alcohol, sex, or in the ultimate, suicide, which I see as simply the most desperate attempt to find freedom from these ghastly realities. But wait! What if we could somehow find the strength to face them head-on and learn to ultimately enjoy our lives so that thoughts and acts of desperation are left behind for good?

My friend, Savior, and Lord, Jesus, has taught me to do just that. You too can learn to live in such a way that every circumstance, no matter how painful, is viewed as an opportunity to develop even more intimacy with Jesus. This life is but a template for the next. The degree of intimacy that we have with Him in this life is the degree to which we will enjoy Him for all eternity in the afterlife. God has brought me from years of languishing in suicidal depression, even prior to the spinal cord injury, to revisiting hope, dreams, and life anew afterwards.

Mine is not the only one: the world is full of tragedy. The truth of our particular issues can be harsh indeed. Maybe you've just lost a loved one, such as a child, a spouse, or a close friend. Maybe you just received a phone call from the doctor that was very bad news. Maybe you've been in an accident that nearly claimed your life. Real life is hard! Maybe you've even gotten to a point where you've found that you have come to the end of yourself, of God, and of those around you; where you and those on whom you rely are so spent and weatherworn that you need to seek other sources of encouragement. Stick with me. That's what this book is all about.

Learning to live in Jesus is not just a decision. Becoming born-again is only the beginning. You can learn a way of life that is contrary to the one you had previously. Read on, and look what Paul wrote from a prison cell:

> I know what it is to be in need, and I know what it is to have
> plenty. I have learned the secret of being content in any and every

situation, whether well fed or hungry, whether living in plenty or in want. I can do all this through him who gives me strength. (Philippians 4:12–13)

So finding true contentment can be done!

Jesus is in the moment. I've heard it said that if God were in the past, He would be "I Was" or if He were in the future, He would be "I Will Be." But as you can only find Him in the present, He is "I Am." When it comes right down to it, you only ever have this moment. In light of this, it is important that you become discerning enough in the here and now to hear His still, small voice speaking His whisper to you as you go through your most precious day. How do you do that? Through studying the scripture daily and through saturating the Spirit within you with godly music, literature, radio and television, even having downtime with loved ones. Exercising discipline, we need to forsake worldly or ungodly stimuli in general. Now, you cannot possibly forgo *all* ungodly influences merely because you live in a fallen world. I only suggest that when you can, choose wisely that to which your ears and eyes are exposed. You may like, for instance, to watch the news or read a newspaper to keep yourself informed about what is going on in the world, but you should be extra-vigilant to choose wisely. For example, do you choose a movie that compromises your beliefs, repeatedly uses the name of the Lord in vain, or has numerous curse words or licentious scenes in it? I say again: you need to choose very carefully that to which your eyes and ears are exposed. Once the ungodly stimulus has entered into you, it's in there, and there's no taking it back. I do believe that such stimuli dulls our spiritual acuity. Nowadays, there are so many godly, uplifting movies and even TV programs. We do have choices.

We only get one time around. This one life of yours and mine is more about making choices than perhaps we acknowledge. It's about choosing to have a certain attitude, choosing whether or not to open up to change, choosing to look to others or to rely on our own strength and self-sufficiency, or choosing to lean into a God who promises His power, presence, and rest to anyone who will come to Him (Matthew 11:28–30). Don't know about you, but I have a tendency to rely on myself a lot more than I think I should. Maybe, if you're truly honest, you can relate to this.

God's Bible states that the supernatural world of demons and the devil is real. Some do not believe in the devil; that makes him happy. As long as he can blind people to the reality of his existence, they are no threat to him. Not believing in the devil does not negate his existence. The devil is a very real being in the unseen realm who will do his utmost to prevent people from seeing the truth about Jesus, and/or get them to turn away from God in discouragement and disillusionment. Let's look at the fall of man in the garden of Eden to further illustrate my point.

The devil took the form of a serpent and lured Eve to eat of the forbidden fruit that God warned would cause death if consumed. This story is familiar to us.

Satan said to Eve, regarding her eating the fruit, "You will not surely die. For God knows that in the day you eat of it your eyes will be opened, and you will be like God, knowing good and evil" (Genesis 3:4–5 NKJV). Looking more carefully at the works of the devil in this instance, we can see that he cast doubt in Eve's mind about what God had actually said to her in his earlier warning.

The Bible reveals that that's how the devil works: casting doubt, causing confusion, and muddying the mind. Joyce Meyer wrote a best-selling book called *Battlefield of the Mind.* Indeed, there is a war going on in each one of us that involves real, definite, and particular choices, as I've said.

Not only do we, as Christians, need to contend with Satan, but there is an *intrapersonal* battle going on. "For the flesh lusts against the Spirit, and the Spirit against the flesh; and these are contrary to one another, so that you do not do the things that you wish." (Galatians 5:17 NKJV). As well, we have to deal with conflicts between people. Truly, life is difficult.

God, however, is not some harsh type of character, removed from what happens to you, ready to judge you and pounce on you for your every fault and wrongdoing. Sometimes we can put onto God the parenting we received. Allow me to explain. For instance, if you had an angry and unreasonable father, you may tend to have a hard time accepting that God is loving and really feel that. Or if you had an abandoning parent, you may have a difficult time accepting that God is there for you any and all the time. In my childhood, my father was all of that: angry, unreasonable, and abandoning. He left the family home when I was four. This precipitated a formal separation from my mother, though he came for a short time for visits to the house. Then, he would speak openly of his hatred for my mother in front of the three of us children. For many years after I became a Christian, though I knew in my head that Jesus loved me, to actually *feel* it escaped me; same thing with the feeling that God was always there for me, purely because of the way my father, my male role model, had treated me. God slowly revealed His character to me over a period of years (and continues to do so). Believe me; He is far different from how I first imagined Him. Jesus is generously, extravagantly loving, forgiving, rich in mercy, slow to anger, and full of grace. Do you experience Him as that, or are you burdened by hurts from your past that hinder your relating to God?

I believe God has a great and real sense of humor. I recall the story in the book *The Shack* by William Paul Young that speaks of his human allegorical representatives of the three persons of the Trinity—God the Father; Jesus Christ, His Son; and the Holy Spirit—cooking together in a kitchen. A bowl is dropped, and food splatters everywhere. Instead of condemning, cursing, and blaming one another in loud bursts of anger, they all break out into howling laughter! This struck a particular chord with me, as tempers would flare up easily if something like that happened in our house when I was young. There would be yelling and blaming; these would be first on the agenda. In fact, my home growing up was so fraught with these that there was little room for humor or laughter. I love how Mr. Young wonderfully used this simple illustration to reflect the loving and caring nature of the Triune God in relationship with one another, the fun side, the lighter side.

Whether it's light or heavy, Jesus said, "The truth will set you free" (John 8:32). There is freedom of a spiritual kind to be found in the embracing of all truth, no matter how easy or how tough that may be to do, including the proven facts that life is difficult and is pain.

Join me in the next chapter, as I will delve even more deeply into these two truths. It is in living with these concepts firmly planted within us as foundational and consistent facts that we, ironically, can feel free of their grip. Allow me to explain.

CHAPTER TWO

MORE ON LIFE

hen trouble comes, if we have incorporated the truths that life is difficult and painful deep within us, we can more readily accept difficulty, even profound agony, not only as something that merely *is* but as something to be *expected*. When we do this, we will find ourselves having the strength and resilience to bounce back more quickly, as we realize that to have trouble—deep trouble—is just par for the course and a normal part of life, instead of a ghastly, unwelcome intruder. Jesus put it this way: "In this world you will have trouble. But take heart! I have overcome the world" (John 16:33). Notice here that Jesus speaks of Himself as *the* solution. Relying on and trusting Him, whatever the circumstances, helps us not to crumble under the weight of even relentless, excruciating anguish.

I had a situation where a relative from my family of origin took me to court, not once but twice.

In the first instance, I won and was given the power to make all medical decisions for my ailing father with Alzheimer's and to place him in a long-term care home. The second time we went to court, my relative wanted full control over Dad and was not content to let me be responsible for him in the capacities assigned to me. And though this particular relative had not held a job (paying or otherwise) in more than thirty years, this person persisted in his or her efforts to attain full control over my dad. (Incidentally, I won the second time as well.)

Jesus stood beside me through these agonizing ordeals, through it all, as He so faithfully promises to do for all who trust in Him. I'm sure you have had your fair share of tortuous situations, and in hindsight, saw the faithful hand of God bringing you through.

Jesus is *the* solution! He is enough!

Trouble hits everyone on the planet. I've heard it said that if you're not in a trial, you are about to enter one or are just coming out of one. I've also heard it said that if you're not bothering the devil, he won't bother you. In other words, if you are determined to make your work count for eternity, and you set to working as to God and not as unto "human masters" (Colossians 3:23), you can bet Satan hates you and will try to make you into a defeated follower of Christ by throwing countless trials your way.

The devil loves to try to steal our joy and put us into depression and despair. Ultimately, Satan is so pleased when, giving in to his barrage of negativity, we find ourselves at our lowest and, in desperation, try to take our own lives. He's all about destruction, whereas Jesus is the author of life.

When it comes time for me to pass from this earth, I seek to end well. We don't choose how we start—some begin well and finish poorly; some begin in poverty, perhaps on many levels, but somehow find the strength to finish with dignity and honor.

Jesus speaks of His heaven:

> God will wipe away every tear from … [our] eyes; there shall be no more death, nor sorrow, nor crying.
>
> There shall be no more pain, for the former things have passed away. … Behold, I make all things new. … these words are true and faithful. (Revelation 21:4–5 NKJV)

Hallelujah! Personally, I can't wait! It's not that this life is intolerable; quite the contrary. I just know that the joys I experience here on earth will not compare with the joys and pleasures I will find in heaven. For now—and as long as we live—we will face trials here on earth. Then, all pain will cease, and bliss will take its place—forever! Our minds cannot conceive of it.

Jesus said, "Whoever wants to be my disciple must deny themselves and take up their cross daily and follow me" (Luke 9:23). Dietrich Bonhoeffer, the famous theologian who was assassinated because it was found that he was involved in a plot to kill Hitler, wrote a book called *The Cost of Discipleship*. In it, he speaks of "Costly Grace." "It is costly because it costs a man his life, and it is grace because it gives a man the only true life."[1]

To die to self is no easy or simple task. To deny self and seek to please God only can be arduous. We must be prepared to seek God's face above all else. "But seek first his kingdom and his righteousness, and all these things will be given to you as well" (Matthew 6:33). This is another example of the extravagant love of Jesus.

In one way, it's not easy living as a Christian; in another, it's the easiest way to live, to surrender all our burdens up to Christ and let Him carry us, as in "Footprints" by Margaret Fishback Powers. In that piece of prose, the author comes to realize that in her darkest and most desperate times, God carried her. We can come to Him with all our heaviness. Look at other words of promise made by Jesus in verses to which I alluded earlier:

> Come to me all you who are weary and burdened, and I will give you rest.
>
> Take my yoke upon you and learn from me, for I am gentle and humble in heart, and you will find rest for your souls.
>
> For my yoke is easy and my burden is light. (Matthew 11:28–30)

A yoke is a large, heavy, and bulky piece of wood that is strapped to oxen so they might haul certain items. Jesus, on the other hand, gives us a yoke that is easy to handle. Indeed, His Spirit is light, and He can give us a lighthearted demeanor, even in the face of deep trials. I have some Christian friends with whom I joke and make puns. There is an appropriate lightness, even when we may be dealing with heavy issues.

Getting back to Adam and Eve, as a result of their disobedience in the garden of Eden, God said to Adam, "Cursed is the ground because of you; through *painful toil* you will eat of it all the days of your life" (Genesis 3:17b, italics mine). We were destined from the days of the fall in Eden to experience exhaustion and weariness of body, mind, and soul, purely because of the introduction of sin at that time. It's therefore even more beautiful that Jesus promises rest for all who come to Him. He said, however, that it would not be easy:

> Enter through the narrow gate. For wide is the gate and broad is the road that leads to destruction, and many enter through it.
>
> But small is the gate and narrow the road that leads to life, and only a few find it. (Matthew 7:13–14)

Once again, Jesus promises hardship.
More words of Jesus:

> Therefore do not worry about tomorrow, for tomorrow will worry about itself. Each day has enough trouble of its own. (Matthew 6:34)

Again, more promises of difficulty. But there is hope. Look at even more words of Jesus:

> The thief comes only to steal and kill and destroy; I have come that they may have life and have it to the full. (John 10:10)

I not only want to end well, but I want to have that "full" life here on earth that Jesus promised here. Let's look to Paul:

> Be very careful, then, how you live—not as unwise but as wise,
> making the most of every opportunity, because the days are evil.
>
> Therefore do not be foolish, but understand what the Lord's will
> is. (Ephesians 5:15–17)

The days became evil with the fall of Adam and Eve. Again, face it or
not, we will not cease to need to "be very careful" until God calls us home.
A daunting prospect? God tests us and our faith throughout life, but when we
come to really know Him and serve Him, He makes it a joy. In fact, He provides
joy that acts as a buoy—incredibly, even in the darkest trial, to anyone walking
in the Spirit. (In order to "walk in the Spirit," we need to seek God daily at
every crossroads in our day, asking for His direction.) As we do this, we can
also be testing the spirits (1 John 4:1–3). When applied, this practice can help
in sifting through the many voices or influences that tend to nudge or pull us
this way or that.

Getting back to Ephesians 5:15–17, quoted above—these verses speak of
"understand[ing] what the Lord's will is." If we are, in fact, very careful,
listening for and actively seeking His still, small voice as we travel through our
day, we can learn to decipher His guidance—not perfectly, mind you (we are
prone to making mistakes; it's just in our nature) but with discernment. Jesus
said that if we seek, we *will* find (Matthew 7:7).

Dr. Nabeel Qureshi wrote about his conversion from Islam to Christianity
in his book, *Seeking Allah, Finding Jesus,* highlighting that God *can* be found
by *anyone* who seeks Him sincerely. I gave that book, with a letter attached,
to a couple of Muslim families who are my neighbors. One took the book; the
other did not, though the one who received it remained in their faith.

We can also set up goals for ourselves. It's good to set goals. Setting goals
can give a sense of direction in itself. It causes us to push forward and when we
achieve our goal, we can have a sense of accomplishment. However, someone
once said, "Be careful what you dream. It might just come true." Some folks

spend their whole lives chasing a goal; when they finally realize it, its acquisition turns out to be bittersweet in nature.

Life, with both its surprisingly challenging highs and its devastating lows, can get so complicated and just plain tough that even the most stable and steadiest of minds can find their thoughts veering towards heaven. Again, a place where there is "no more death or mourning or crying or pain" (Revelation 21:4) is very attractive indeed, especially when the walls start to close in on us as we forage through this painful, difficult, and oftentimes messy life. We need to live this life and face our pain, all the while having thoughts of heaven stashed deeply in our minds. Only then can we stand a chance to do as James suggests, "Consider it pure joy, my brothers and sisters, whenever you face trials of many kinds, because you know that the testing of your faith produces perseverance" (James 1:2–3). Can we look at our trials in such a way as to see that joy can, in fact, be found in them? For instance, we can know that all our perseverance in this life will be rewarded in the next. Certainly, that is cause for joy! I will speak more on trials in the next couple of chapters.

CHAPTER THREE

TRIALS – PART 1

It's possible to be of the frame of mind that God owes us something, that somehow, because we are persevering through trials with Jesus, we should be earning "brownie points" with God, and that He should make our lives go smoothly, according to *our* will or plan. Ever felt that way? God, in His sovereignty, has the first and last word on what happens to all of us. Sometimes what He allows or wills is far from what we want; it goes against the grain, in fact, and throws a huge monkey wrench into *our* plans.

There's no escaping it; when this happens, life once again proves itself to be difficult and painful. We can be humbled, and find ourselves having to come back to Him, to acknowledge and acquiesce to His will for our lives, even if that includes deep suffering. I'm reminded of Jesus's agony in the garden of Gethsemane when *He* acquiesced by saying, "My Father, if it is possible, may this cup be taken from me. Yet not as I will, but as you will" (Matthew 26:39). He didn't want to face the cross but chose to do the will of His Father.

Someone might say, "Yeah, but He was God!" I think the following verses are clear:

> If you suffer … and … endure it, this is commendable before God. To this you were called, because Christ suffered for you, leaving you an example, that you should follow in his steps. (1 Peter 2:20–21)

Jesus showed the way in which we are to walk. Sometimes we plod merrily ahead with our day, not realizing that God has His plan for it as well. When the two don't match up, and we are blown way off course, we are tempted to curse and fuss and fume. It is at such times that we need to dig deep; maybe think of what we have in this part of the world—clean running hot and cold water at our beck and call, food stores on every corner, not to mention churches. Many who live elsewhere do not. The challenges we experience are real—don't get me wrong—but putting more of a global spin on them can help to take the sting out of them.

Slowly, over time, as we see God working in and through our troubles, He, in His faithfulness, can reveal Himself again and again to be bigger than the trial He has allowed. Indeed, He is bigger than we are (Isaiah 55:8–9) and perhaps bigger than we thought He was. When we see His hand faithfully guiding us to a shore of safety or helping us with something so very difficult, we can see, in hindsight, that He is so big and great. He is considerably bigger than any circumstances in which we find ourselves. He can handle any trial we may face. It only takes a horrific diagnosis from the doctor, or one bad storm that does profound damage to our home, or the sudden death of a loved one to drive us to our knees. In the face of horror from whatever source, there is One who understands our pain. He will be there for us, in and through it. He even may cause us to come around and eventually be grateful for the very devastation that flattened us in the first place. He did it for me; He can do it for you.

As we come to embrace the truth of our situations, grieve, and let go of any losses (which can be a very laborious process, perhaps even requiring years, depending on the situation), God proceeds to restore and fortify our faith, building it up even stronger than it had been prior to our ordeal. In *The Problem of Pain,* C. S. Lewis writes,

> We can ignore even pleasure. But pain insists upon being attended to. God whispers to us in our pleasures, speaks in our conscience, but shouts in our pains: it is his megaphone to rouse a deaf world.[2]

Pain, then, is not only used to call you closer to Jesus, but it affects those around you. Those who witness the way you handle it can be drawn to Him. Are you letting God use your anguish? Nearly everybody has some sort of anguish in his or her life, whether it pertains to relatives, friends, or coworkers; health issues; or financial struggles, as examples. Are you reaching out, even in the midst of your trial, to be a walking testimony and witness for Jesus? People are watching you, Christians and non-Christians alike.

Are you helping spread the Word, whether through your actions or words? You might groan here because none of us like to risk rejection. Realize, however, that it was because the disciples cared more about hurting, lost souls and their eventual separation forever from all that is love than about their own feelings. They shared way back, and that witnessing went on from one generation to the next, so that you presently have Jesus in your heart.

The late preacher E. V. Hill used to say that we are it. God has chosen "no one and nothin' else!" We, as Christians, hold within us the knowledge of what it takes to change someone's eternal destiny. If you knew the cure for cancer, would you keep it to yourself? We have the cure for something much worse than cancer—everlasting punishment.

It's not so easily done sometimes. Some of us are gifted in witnessing, and others are not, but still, God says, "Always be prepared to give an answer to everyone who asks you to give the reason for the hope that you have. But do this with gentleness and respect, keeping a clear conscience" (1 Peter 3:15b–16a). Groan as you might, I'll say it again: we're it; you're it. You may consider witnessing to be a trial, but there is great joy to be had in helping lead a wounded soul in the Sinner's Prayer! Since my wheelchair, I have had that privilege over seventy times!

CHAPTER FOUR
TRIALS – PART 2

*O*nly Jesus can turn your trials into something beautiful. In time, you can find yourself ministering to the very folks who are going through what you have been through. You can become a walking example of what victory in Jesus looks like.

> Praise be to the God and Father of our Lord Jesus Christ, the Father of compassion and the God of all comfort, who comforts us in all our troubles, so that we can comfort those in any trouble with the comfort we ourselves receive from God. (2 Corinthians 1:3–4)

That's Jesus at His very best. But you need to accept your pain, your situation as it is, in order to be used by God in such a way. Personally, I'd rather take the spiritual strength and freedom that comes with the embracing of the truths of my own personal trials, however painful, as well as the truth of the availability of God's help in all its bigness, than to end up being blindsided for lack of preparation when my time comes to meet Him.

> People are destined to die once, and after that to face judgment. (Hebrews 9:27)

Only God knows when our time is over here on earth. I say again--are you ready for that day?

Joni Eareckson Tada suggests we embrace our trials as friends. Jesus can give us the strength, the help, to do this as we heed His call to us to be our best friend. God urges us to shun idolatry of every kind. Someone might say, "I'm not into idolatry. I don't worship statues or anything like that." Ah, but do you hold anything in more esteem or love anything more than you love the Savior? An idol, then, is anything we put higher than and above God in our lives. That could be a person, such as a parent, spouse, or significant other; or it could be a pet or a thing, like a car or a house; or it could even be a hobby, a habit, or a practice of some sort—even work. I ask you: do you make spending time alone with Jesus, as prolific author and pastor Dr. Charles Stanley has said, the number-one priority in your life? I would imagine this would be especially challenging for those who are married. Though I've never had a spouse, it speaks to common sense that each individual in a couple should carve out quiet time alone with the Savior; they should seek to get their spiritual goodies from Him and then minister to each other from the overflow.

God communicates with us in so many ways, in our quiet times with Him and the Bible, but also through people; through that conviction and other spiritual nudges; through books, music, creation, or dreams; through all sorts of circumstances.

The best way we can communicate with God regarding the trials we face is through prayer. As the song says,

> What a friend we have in Jesus,
> All our sins and griefs to bear!
> What a privilege to carry
> Everything to God in prayer!

> O what peace we often forfeit,
> O what needless pain we bear,
> All because we do not carry
> Everything to God in prayer!

Indeed, we are called to "pray continually" (1 Thessalonians 5:17). While I will speak more on prayer in later chapters, suffice it to say here that prayer is like spiritual therapy and can be healing like nothing else. After watching the movie *The War Room*, I revamped and extended my personal prayer time. I encourage you to take the time to watch it, and see if it doesn't inspire you also to renovate *your* prayer time.

With Jesus being omniscient, someone might ask: why pray when He knows it all anyway? Because God yearns to develop profound intimacy with His followers, and prayer is the main way to do that.

He knows we need intimacy with Him; in fact, He can relate to us in every way:

> For we do not have a high priest who is unable to empathize with
> our weaknesses, but we have one who has been tempted in every
> way, just as we are—yet he did not sin. (Hebrews 4:15)

He knows weakness of every kind, yet He never made a mistake! That speaks to His 100 percent humanity, as well as His 100 percent divinity. He understands us more deeply than even our good friends or spouses can, even more than we can understand ourselves. He knows fully what we are going through. Our trials and circumstances may not change, but He is a master of doing actual "heart surgery," adjusting our attitudes and the way we see our situations. Don't doubt that He can do it for you as well. However, we do have a part to play.

Jesus's said, "Ask and it will be given to you; seek and you will find; knock and the door will be opened to you" (Matthew 7:7). Dr. Charles Stanley says that the verbs in this verse in the original Greek are written in such an imperative form as to mean, "Ask and keep on asking"; "Seek and keep on seeking"; "Knock and keep on knocking." That is our work. Persevering in this way, we are not only fed in every way, but we again build that necessary intimacy with Jesus.

Christian recording artist Fernando Ortega sings that it is his darkest fear "to come home a stranger." Certainly, we offer up prayers and petitions; I also think it pleases God when we just simply abide in His presence.

Be still and know that I am God. (Psalm 46:10)

Just sitting and soaking in His presence can be very healing. I have a friend who makes a regular practice of sitting in the silence and abiding with Jesus. I have witnessed his being healed of anxiety, to a large degree, because of this very practice.

We are called not only to be still with Jesus but also to remain in Him.

I am the vine; you are the branches. If you remain in me and I in you, you will bear much fruit. (John 15:5)

The branch cannot produce the fruit (Galatians 5:22–23) on its own, but the branch that stays attached to the vine will. Truly, walking closely with Jesus, in and through our trials, is the answer for all of us.

CHAPTER FIVE

ALL THINGS
SPIRITUAL – PART 1

There are two main spiritual forces in the world. Jesus stood firm against the devil (Matthew 4:1–11), and He admonishes us to do so as well:

> Be alert and of sober mind. Your enemy the devil prowls around like a roaring lion looking for someone to devour.

> Resist him, standing firm in the faith, because you know that the family of believers throughout the world is undergoing the same kind of sufferings. (1 Peter 5:8–9)

In His strength, we too can be victorious over our enemy.

Satan has a whole slew of demonic cohorts that work for and with him. The apostle Paul says this, "For our struggle is not against flesh and blood, but against the rulers, against the authorities, against the powers of this dark world and against the spiritual forces of evil in the heavenly realms" (Ephesians 6:12). To rephrase, then, our battles are not with other human beings, as it might first appear on the surface. The battles are on a deeper level, in the spiritual realm. If a particular person is irking you, remember that forces are at work that influence that person to behave the way he or she does, and prayer can address that.

As we choose to seriously seek Jesus and come to know Him more intimately,

His bigness and our helplessness truly become evident. Again, the many horrific weather stories from all over the world that cause such devastation and loss of life are testaments to this. Singer/songwriter James Taylor sings about two ants dancing on a blade of grass: "That's you and me, baby. We're so small, and the world's so vast."

Speaking of music, I have a favorite song of worship by recording artist Fernando Ortega. He sings "Give Me Jesus." In the morning when I rise, when I am alone, and when I come to die, give me Jesus. Someone has said that we don't know the terror of actually facing physical death until we go through it. I believe, however, that it can also be the deepest, most holy transition with Him.

Jesus simply asks that you come to Him, especially when the burdens of life weigh you down so much that you wonder if it's all worth it—if you're worth the toil. You are; you are infinitely precious. Don't allow the enemy to tell you anything different. We are all creations of God; we are worthy of treating ourselves well, worthy of accepting all He has to offer. Again, though, we must choose to go to Him.

Certainly, we can get into situations that stem from circumstances out of our control. Sometimes the only thing we *can* control is our reaction to them. Yes, we can find ourselves in difficult circumstances, but some people are just plain difficult.

On the book cover of an earlier edition of *The Sociopath Next Door*, psychologist Dr. Martha Stout asks, "Who is the devil you know?" This was an eye-opening book for me in terms of understanding difficult people.

You might think that the word *sociopath* only describes a mass murderer or a serial killer, a Paul Bernardo or an Adolf Hitler. However, Stout points out that in the general population, one in twenty-five people is a sociopath. These are people who often have good jobs, are highly influential, and are very charismatic with powerful personalities, but they are also entirely lacking in conscience. The book was recommended to me in order to help me deal with a particularly difficult person in my life. I found it offered good insight and helped me a great deal.

Sociopaths, Stout writes, can be highly manipulative, intelligent, and convincing. She comments that the devil and God are almost indistinguishable. Though she does not profess to have a faith of her own, she does show remarkable insight here. We need knowledge and keen discernment to be able to identify the two. Paul himself speaks of "false apostles, deceitful workers, masquerading as apostles of Christ. And no wonder, for Satan himself masquerades as an angel of light. It is not surprising, then, if his servants also masquerade as servants of righteousness. Their end will be what their actions deserve" (2 Corinthians 11:13–15).

Stout offers help in recognizing Satan. She says "if there is a devil," he would have us feel very sorry for him, explaining that sociopaths play on the sympathy of good people. In pointing this out, I'm not saying here that we should not have sympathy for people—quite the contrary—but we are to pick and choose carefully those to whom we give it, recognizing that decisions—choices again—to act in a certain way have been made all along. To sum up regarding Stout's book, she arms the reader to recognize and contend with a very dangerous and cunningly convincing sect of society.

We all need to guard our hearts above all else (Proverbs 4:23)—it is the foundation of life. Only you can keep yourself safe and keep up proper boundaries. (Maybe you don't know what I mean by the term *boundaries*; they are invisible dividing lines between people. As boundaries are let down in any healthy relationship over time, the two people involved can find deeper trust and fulfillment.) Learning to guard our hearts, then, is one awesome responsibility. Jesus calls us to stay faithful to Him:

> My eyes will be on the faithful in the land, that they may dwell with me; the one whose walk is blameless will minister to me. (Psalm 101:6)

These are particularly precious words to me. It says we can actually provide solace to the Lord by making godly choices in our everyday lives. We honor

Him by choosing to look to Him not only throughout our daily walk but by choosing to give Him the control, no matter how seemingly endless and excruciating our journey may be, not only in general, but also as to how and when we leave this world. Death is a one-shot deal; I will argue that it needs to be left in the hands of the Creator. Just as you had absolutely no say in your creation, the time and means of your death needs to be left to Jesus.

CHAPTER SIX

ALL THINGS
SPIRITUAL – PART 2

We can glean strength in our journey by studying Jesus's.

He went to the garden of Gethsemane prior to His crucifixion. There, in deep anguish, He said, "My soul is overwhelmed with sorrow to the point of death" (Matthew 26:38). He begged His Father in His agony, pleading with Him, "My Father, if it is possible, may this cup be taken from me" (Matthew 26:39).

Again, Jesus chose to face the reality, the truth of His Father's will for Him—crucifixion on a cruel Roman cross, though He had done nothing wrong. Further, Jesus shouldered the weight of all human sin—past, present, and future—as well as separation from the Father, something Christ had never known before, in saying, "Yet not as I will, but as you will" (Matthew 26:39). Can we make that our prayer, especially in times of profound pain and especially when thoughts of ending our lives come to mind? Incidentally, we should recognize that such thoughts come directly from Satan and are not of God, so we should not entertain them.

God provided Jesus as the ultimate example for us to emulate but also the apostle Paul (Galatians 4:12; 1 Corinthians 11:1), who said, "I eagerly expect and hope that I will in no way be ashamed, but will have sufficient courage so that now as always Christ will be exalted in my body, whether by life or by death" (Philippians 1:20). Can we say that? Can we truly say that?

Paul was a prolific author. He wrote many books of the New Testament. The Holy Spirit used such men to pen His words to humankind. Listen again to Paul as He speaks specifically to followers of Christ:

> Do you not know that your bodies are temples of the Holy Spirit, who is in you, whom you have received from God?
>
> You are not your own; you were bought at a price.
>
> Therefore honor God with your bodies. (1 Corinthians 6:19–20)

To honor God with your body is to realize that you are worthy of caring for it well—to feed it good things, to rest and exercise in balanced amounts. If you are finding it difficult to do these things, are feeling down and are in fact in a position where you have come to the end of yourself and have had serious thoughts of suicide, get yourself to the hospital (you need trained medical professionals around you), and remember these most precious words: that it is the devil who comes to steal and kill and destroy. It is Jesus who came that we may have life and have it in all its fullness (John 10:10).

A few years ago, I befriended a gentleman who was acutely suicidal and had been for some time. I encouraged him to go to the hospital. He refused. Some days, I spent about six hours with him on the phone. I became his lifeline. I eventually developed caregiver fatigue and was about to plunge into mental sickness myself, so I was forced to say goodbye to this gentleman. His sister emailed me, months later, to tell me that he had killed himself the day after I said goodbye to him. Take my suggestion seriously. The hospital is a healing place.

Remember that tough times don't last; tough people do. Cling to His promises. This verse has many: "Even to your old age and gray hairs I am he, I am he who will sustain you. I have made you and I will carry you; I will sustain you and I will rescue you" (Isaiah 46:4).

More of His promises: Paul said, "Now if we are children, then we are heirs—heirs of God and co-heirs with Christ, if indeed we share in his sufferings in order that we may also share in his glory" (Romans 8:17). We are heirs of God. Take a moment to think about that. We will one day inherit all God's riches. Certainly, that is worth hanging on for! It is my wish to say with Paul, "I have fought the good fight, I have finished the race, I have kept the faith" (2 Timothy 4:7). Is it yours?

Elsewhere in scripture, Paul cries out, "I want to know Christ—yes, to know the power of his resurrection and participation in his sufferings, becoming like him in his death, and so, somehow, attaining to the resurrection from the dead" (Philippians 3:10–11). Paul speaks here of the attitude of choosing to share in Christ's sufferings, not merely grudgingly carrying on because we feel we *have to* but willingly entering into them—actually choosing to do that. I have slowly come to see that God is faithful in giving me the strength to share in Christ's sufferings and that I am entirely dependent on Him to provide for me in that way. Much of what God does and allows is truly a mystery to me. Mother Teresa once said that she would have many questions when she meets Jesus in heaven.

My very favorite verse in all scripture is Isaiah 55:8:

"For my thoughts are not your thoughts, neither are your ways my ways," declares the Lord.

Why God allows certain folk to suffer continually is beyond me, but I do know that He is in control and that He is sovereign over all that happens to us.

I truly believe that when I face Jesus on my judgment day, God will finally reveal His unfathomable, incomprehensible, eternal perspective to me, the one that eluded my limited, finite mind while I was here on earth. All will be made clear. At that time, I will rejoice and thank Him for putting me through the trials He did. We will never fully understand Him in this life. In the meantime, we can choose to rest in faith, enter into His sufferings, and pray for patience that we might hold on 'til that day when we do see Him face-to-face.

Borrowing again from Paul:

We know that the whole creation has been groaning as in the pains of childbirth right up to the present time.

Not only so, but we ourselves, who have the firstfruits of the Spirit, groan inwardly as we wait eagerly for our adoption to sonship, the redemption of our bodies.

For in this hope we were saved. But hope that is seen is no hope at all. Who hopes for what they already have?

But if we hope for what we do not yet have, we wait for it patiently. (Romans 8:22–25)

Though we don't often like to admit it, much of life is about waiting—waiting in the checkout line, waiting for the bus, waiting for the light to change, waiting for the right person to be our spouse, waiting for the return of Christ. In the next couple of chapters, we will look more closely at the fruit of patience.

CHAPTER SEVEN
PATIENCE—PART 1

Growth is measured over time. We talk about the growth of a child, for instance, not in terms of a daily change but over a period of time. Often, it's a span of many months, or perhaps years that go by before we can say, "My, that child has really grown." So it is with adults on the spiritual level. Growth is a process, and change is often slow and minute, difficult to measure. We may need those close to us to comment on the changes they have seen in us; it can be difficult for us to see in ourselves.

God says, "Love is patient, love is kind..." (1 Corinthians 13:4). He lists *patient* first of all because He knows how demanding we sometimes can be of Him, of others, and especially of ourselves. I can require so much from myself, and I can be so judgmental of others I just see on the street. We need to ease up on everyone, including ourselves. We need to be patient and careful with regard to our own energies and when relating to others.

My roommate in the institution, a wise, elderly woman, once said to me, "God works slow but sure." Trust that over time, as you are patient, you will see your suffering differently than you might see it today. Healing is not an event but a process—sometimes a laborious and lengthy one at that. It took over three years of my being suicidal when I was new to the wheelchair for the Lord to raise me up above those dark feelings. God knows how impatient we are to get out of the pain we are currently in. Submitting daily to what He is allowing in our lives, to His will, calls for patient endurance (Revelation 14:12) in order for Him to create and hone in us that character of love.

Christian recording artist Steve Bell sings that we may be lonely and that it's a hard road making us holy, but in the long run, there will be glory. In other words, "Hang in there! It'll all be worth it in the end."

On *His* road to glory, Jesus said to his disciples in the garden of Gethsemane, "Watch and pray so that you will not fall into temptation. The spirit is willing, but the flesh is weak" (Matthew 26:41). As Jesus called his disciples to be patient and enduring in prayer, so it is with us. The devil comes at us with temptation (James 1:13). If we are careful and discerning, we can recognize when he is doing this, head him off at the pass, and reach for Jesus. Jesus can lead us to triumph over that temptation, providing us with supernatural power not to succumb to Satan's icy fingers of lure. Jesus had asked His followers to pray, but they gave in. Perhaps they started to pray but ended up dozing off. How often has that happened to us?

Prayer involves discipline; we need to carve out a specific block of time in our busy days to spend alone with Jesus. Satan is good at influencing me—to the point that my quiet time gets squeezed out of my day. Maybe you can relate. We need to be extra vigilant not let this happen. And we need to be patient and loving with ourselves when it does. We are but human—frail and fragile.

Can you imagine someone you love sitting on your couch, wishing to spend time with you, while you busy yourself around the house and ignore this person altogether? Now imagine that this person is the third person of the Trinity, the Holy Spirit. I can't help but think that His feelings would be hurt. Yet He is patient with us. He understands—He really does—and He forgives. All the same, can you and I try to be more mindful of the emotional reactions of God toward all we say and do?

When friends and/or family desert us, pangs of loneliness can draw us into seeking the Prince of Peace and His Word more often and with more depth. Each day, I take my Bible (or at least I try) and my journal, and I interact with the Word and with Jesus in a dialogue that is so healing. He is there for us, no matter what we go through, to whatever depth we choose to pursue Him. He is faithful, friend. You can trust Him.

Only you can choose to trust God, turning away from discouragement and despair. When you are tempted toward discouragement, instead of visiting and revisiting your pain, try to refocus and think of the blessings, even in your suffering—what you've learned from it, how it's drawn you to Him in a deeper way, how it has the capacity to provide an even richer and deeper gratitude reservoir. He will use your pain as a teacher if you can be patient. Please be patient, and rest assured that God is at work.

Preacher John Hagee says that when you're down to nothing, God is up to something. Look what God did through a teenager, Joni Eareckson Tada, who made the mistake of diving into shallow water; this accident cost her the use of her legs and her hands. Despite this, she eventually founded one of the largest ministries to the disabled in North America, Joni and Friends. She has been a source of help and encouragement to many, including me.

As well, Jesus was down to nothing by worldly standards, sentenced to die by crucifixion between two common criminals. But three days later, God provided the way of redemption for the entire human race. The disciples had to be patient, waiting for Sunday to come, until they saw their risen Savior.

And imagine the patience of God the Father in watching His only Son grow from a helpless baby, with sin-prone human parents, to a man, and then watching at a distance, not intervening or rescuing (as we sometimes hope He would do with us), as Jesus was humiliated, tortured, and killed slowly in excruciating pain. The Father waited years, only to watch as His beloved Son was crucified for you and for me. God the Father knew just what the deep, incredible suffering of Jesus was to achieve. If you have experienced physical or psychological abuse, let me say how sorry I am that you had to endure that first of all; then, please recall how Jesus endured mockery and physical beatings (Matthew 27:27–31). Rest assured that He knows your pain. Trust that He has divine purposes for all our suffering, just as the Father had divine purposes for the suffering of Jesus.

Sometimes, though, it's hard to trust. The late preacher Dr. Ravi Zacharias said that the problem is not that God is not able to provide for us; the problem is that we don't trust Him to do just that. We can turn away from God, especially when deep trials come, and sit in self-pity (a dead-end road, by the way) or pummel Him with *why* questions, not being satisfied until we have *the* answer for which we are looking. When others mistreat us, we can be quick to blame and curse. Or we can be quick to be understanding and patient with others, even with God. With ourselves, however, this sometimes can be the most difficult hurdle. We can be so loving with others but just plain cruel to ourselves. The devil is happy when he sees this. We can be so vicious to ourselves that we can end up thinking that the best thing would be for us to end our lives. It's not. You have value and worth beyond measure.

Satan can use the deep pain of regret or a relentless, ongoing struggle to wear a person down, and then he plants seeds—thoughts of suicide. He may be at work right now in your heart, trying to erode your precious hope—precious hope that tries to whisper that there will be brighter days. He uses lies such as, "It'll always be this way"; "The situation is hopeless"; "You're hopeless"; and so on. He is called "the accuser of our brothers and sisters" (Revelation 12:10b). Satan is the one who taunts and blames. He was the one at the root of the scapegoating I received as a child. I was made the family scapegoat; my mom had been a scapegoat in her family of origin. As she was unable to find healing for this, she inadvertently, actually quite innocently passed it on to me. I was ostracized, ridiculed, laughed at and made to feel unwelcome in and by my own family. It wasn't until I was in my late teens that I realized I even *had* feelings, as mine had gotten so stuffed way down, out of reach. Again though, this was ultimately Satan's work. My mom didn't know Jesus as her Savior, and doesn't to this day.

The devil is a joy- and strength-stealer; he tries to oppress, whereas God specializes in working in and through seemingly "impossible" situations for the eventual good of those who love Him (Romans 8:28). "With God, all things are possible" (Matthew 19:26b), or, as the song says, "God will make a way where there seems to be no way." But we must watch and wait. It all takes faith and patience.

Author Robert Morgan, in his book, *The Red Sea Rules*, encourages the reader to stay calm and confident in difficult times and give God time to work. I have a friend who admits, "I'm not fond of God's timing," but we must wait patiently for it, as it is perfect. Extending fruits like patience, kindness, and goodness to ourselves can be especially difficult for those who were not consistently treated in like fashion when they were growing up. Regular criticism and harshness from a parent can erode a child's sense of well-being and hope. When such children grow up, they may sit in self-blame and self-flagellation, actually reinforcing the abuse because that is what is so familiar. They may listen to the whispers of the enemy as he berates them, giving fuel to these temptations by dwelling on them. Such folk may find themselves continuing to linger on such thoughts as a form of emotional comfort food.

If you too were abused, I'm so sorry that you had to endure that. Please know, however, that the "tapes" that play in your mind as a result of early mistreatment will go away completely only when you get to heaven and receive a new resurrection body. Though the tapes remain, there is hope. Spiritual discipline helps you to catch the devil when he is using the tapes; you can come to a point where you can recognize that he is tempting you to dwell on such thoughts. You might say, simply, "Away from me, Satan, in Jesus's name." And/ or you might quote scripture, such as, for example, Philippians 1:6 or 1 John 4:4—good verses to memorize, by the way. Satan may begin the negative tapes playing, but, again, it is your choice whether or not you pursue and entertain them. Remember: "For our struggle is … against the spiritual forces of evil in the heavenly realms" (Ephesians 6:12).

CHAPTER EIGHT
PATIENCE—PART 2

Regarding my being the family scapegoat, my family trained me to be a doormat. I grew up without boundaries of any kind. It was in not having them that I realized, much later in life, how truly necessary they are. I encountered a series of predators in my life prior to my developing boundaries. In fact, my very first encounter with a helping professional in my late teens was with a predator. He "groomed" me for two years, earning my trust (in fact, he was the first man who truly listened to me, so I became quite dependent on him). He asked me in what turned out to be our last session, to "describe in as great detail as possible how sexual relations would be between" him and me. Indeed, we are in a war, a war that needs armor:

> Therefore put on the full armor of God, so that when the day of evil comes, you may be able to stand your ground. (Ephesians 6:13)

The best time to put on the armor is in the morning when you get up. If you're like me and are not at your best in the morning, just say, "Suit me up, Lord." He will know what you mean.

My dear dad had a hard time in the morning as well. On that very subject, he memorized (despite his Alzheimer's) an old military song written by Irving Berlin. Dad was a commanding officer in the Royal Canadian Air Force for many years. He used to sing his version of this little ditty, which he called his theme song:

Oh, how I hate to get up in the morning!
Oh, how I long to remain in bed!
And the harshest blow of all is to hear the bugler call,
Ya gotta get up, ya gotta get up, ya gotta get up this morning.

Someday I'm going to murder the bugler.
Someday they're going to find him dead.
I'll amputate his reveille and step upon it heavily,
And spend the rest of my life in bed!

My dad had a great sense of humor. One summer day when I was visiting with him in the hospital because of his Alzheimer's, my T-shirt was riding up a little on my tummy. When I was ready to leave, I said, "I'm gonna take off now, Dad. Okay?" He gently took the edge of my T-shirt and said, "Don't take off; pull down!"

Dad was such a card!

In the early stages of his Alzheimer's, Dad lived in his own house for a number of years. One day when I came to visit him there, out of the blue, he inquired about Jesus and expressed a desire to know Him. Now, I had been praying for this day for twenty-five years. Still, I was shocked! This man, who had built his empire on making money and had had a love of money for so many years, humbled himself, and I had the incredible privilege of helping lead him in a little prayer to invite Jesus to be Lord of his life. He became a Christian in June 2012 in his seventy-ninth year. God caused this camel to go miraculously through the eye of the needle (Matthew 19:24) that day. Between the time of his conversion and his death at age eighty-six, God transformed my father.

This man who was prone to violence when I was little, who left the family when I was four; this man of whom I was deathly afraid all my life became loving, supportive, kind, patient, gentle, and caring. In fact, three years after he accepted Jesus into his heart, he said that I was teaching him how to love.

Dr. Charles Stanley says for a person to find Jesus and spiritual truth after age seventy is one in a million. Dr. Stanley pointed out that such a person would have been steeped in and held on to lies for seventy years, something very difficult to break through. But God did it on that summer day in June 2012 and led me to help my dear dad find peace and love. In October of that year, my dad was taken to the hospital. Despite living in a three-person room in the hospital on a busy ward for nearly four years, when I would ask him how his day went, he would most often respond, "Peaceful and quiet." Truly, only God could have accomplished this.

After his stay in hospital, he went to live in his own room in a good long-term care facility, with many very caring staff. In fact, a staff member once asked Dad if he liked it there. When he said yes, the staff member asked, "And why is that, Ron?" Dad said, "Because of the people." On the Christmas before he passed, he continued to describe his experience as "peaceful" to relatives he spoke to over the phone. God indeed kept him safe and secure in His arms, despite the intense warfare with which Dad had to deal, especially with his Alzheimer's.

Spiritual warfare, something we all face, can be at its most intense within human relationships. The pain of fragmented and broken relationships can drive us to the end of ourselves and tempt us to despair. It is through human relationships, however, that God also provides profound healing. Certainly, it is through people that I have experienced God's love in such powerful ways.

I have a friend who has stuck by me through the many peaks and valleys that we each have encountered individually. Over the years, precious trust has built between this man and me. He's lifted me up when I was tempted to discouragement, and vice versa. We sustained a special bond of friendship while he was dating and maintain it now that he's married. When we speak to each other, there are puns and joking—that lightness I spoke of earlier with the Holy Spirit in the lead. God has used him, in particular, to perform some pretty deep "heart surgery" on me and teach me more of what healthy, Christian friendships are all about.

God poured out His love and kindness to me through this gentleman, and

I, in turn, learned not only to better love myself in a healthy way but to be more patient with myself and with others. What goes around comes around; as this gentleman was patient with me, so I grew in my capacity for patience. He graciously endured my weaknesses. He came to know me so well, in fact, and vice versa, that we could quickly catch one another when we each were headed downward.

> Two are better than one, because they have a good return for their labor: If either of them falls down, one can help the other up. (Ecclesiastes 4:9–10a)

We weren't meant to do this life entirely alone; even Jesus had His disciples.

Patience is required not only in friendships or relationships but in our everyday lives. While it is true that Satan will continue to plant negative thoughts in our minds on a daily basis, until the time we meet God face-to-face, there is hope. Be encouraged that these thoughts can be disregarded with practice. As we train ourselves, they can be virtually squelched as we refuse to entertain them, but again, this takes choice, effort, time—patience.

Dr. Charles Stanley says that God makes a promise. Faith believes it. Hope acknowledges it, and patience quietly waits for it. Helen Keller said that we would never learn to be brave and patient if there were only joy in the world. Philippians 1:6 says, "He who began a good work in you will carry it on to completion until the day of Christ Jesus." We all need to be patient with God, with others, and with ourselves, and trust that God will bring us through. Someone said, "If God brings you to it, He will bring you through it."

Alexander Maclaren, a pastor in Great Britain in the early 1900s, was known as the prince of expository preachers. He said that each of us may be sure that if God sends us on stony paths, He will provide us with strong shoes, and He will not send us out on any journey for which He does not equip us well. I would add, even if the "equipping" takes some time (requires patience).

CHAPTER NINE
HEALTHY SELF-LOVE – PART 1

God is Himself love (1 John 4:16). Jesus teaches, "Love your neighbor as yourself"; this verse is listed many times in scripture for emphasis. This is not a divine suggestion. There are two commandments here. Are you finding the latter of these a tall order? For those who were not treated well when they were growing up, this may be the case, but for those more acquainted with love, likely not.

We are called to a healthy form of self-love, not a negative type of pride, arrogance, or conceit. It was Paul who said,

> Because of these surpassingly great revelations … therefore in order to keep me from becoming conceited, I was given a thorn in my flesh, a messenger of Satan, to torment me. (2 Corinthians 12:7)

While God was revealing wonderfully deep, divine things to Paul, God was aware that the human spirit can grow haughty and puffed up as a result. He wanted to prevent this from happening with Paul, so He gave him a thorn. Rather than choosing to sit and become overwhelmed by despair over his thorn, Paul went straight to the Great Physician in prayer. Despite Paul's pleadings, God chose not to remove the thorn; instead, He chose to provide the power so that Paul could endure it, responding, "My grace is sufficient for you, for my power is made perfect in weakness" (2 Corinthians12:9). Evidently, God had some purpose in having it remain. Don't doubt that about your thorn either.

Back to pride: God says,

"I hate pride and arrogance" (Proverbs 8:13b).

"The Lord detests all the proud of heart" (Proverbs 16:5).

"Pride goes before destruction, a haughty spirit before a fall" (Proverbs 16:18).

Other prophets in the Word say, "God opposes the proud" (James 4:6; 1 Peter 5:5).

Paul said, "Knowledge puffs up while love builds up" (1 Corinthians 8:1).

Jesus Himself exclaimed, "For those who exalt themselves will be humbled, and those who humble themselves will be exalted" (Matthew 23:12). Clearly, then, in scripture, an arrogant form of pride does not bode well with God.

In contrast, however, there is a certain type of pride that is actually encouraged:

> Each one should test their own actions.
>
> Then they can take pride in themselves alone, without comparing themselves to someone else, for each one should carry their own load. (Galatians 6:4–5)

It's okay, then, to love yourself by being proud of your ability to make healthy choices in terms of your emotional, physical, and spiritual well-being or in terms of, say, your accomplishments. In addition, we are to stay focused on God and not divert our attention by comparing ourselves to others. We are each on a unique journey, one with its own individual challenges. Therefore, comparing ourselves to others is unhelpful. We as adults should look only to God in all we do and say.

James says this: "Believers in humble circumstances ought to take pride in his high position" (1:9). This verse is a bit curious. We might gather that from "humble circumstances" comes a lowly position, but even Paul spoke of the weaker member of the body of Christ as being "indispensable" (1 Corinthians 12:22) and that such a one we should "treat with special honor" (1 Corinthians 12:23).

Jesus speaks of the disadvantaged as directly representing Him: "Truly I tell you, whatever you did for one of the least of these brothers and sisters of mine, you did for me" (Matthew 25:40). In other words, if you suffer in some way with a specific weakness, know that God holds you in extra-high esteem, and it's okay to love yourself by taking pride in that particular weakness.

Weakness is frowned upon in the world, but Jesus loves it because it is in this that His power shows up most. Weakness, then, is to be prized.

Paul said,

> I will boast all the more gladly about my weaknesses, so that Christ's power may rest on me.

> That is why, for Christ's sake, I delight in weaknesses, in insults, in hardships, in persecutions, in difficulties. For when I am weak, then I am strong. (2 Corinthians 12:9–10)

Note the wild word there—"delight"! People in Paul's time must have been tempted to think of him as a bit of a nut. Certainly, this word is outlandish, humanly speaking. One might think of the word *endure* or *persevere* when speaking of weaknesses, insults, and hardships. "Delight in" is not a phrase that immediately springs to mind when referring to such things. But Paul was not crazy; he was teaching of the radical love and transformative power of Jesus. Of Jesus Himself, in fact, it has been said that He was either a lunatic, a liar, or Lord, as He said some equally "crazy" things, like, "Love your enemies" (Matthew 5:44), for example.

If you are facing a tormenting thorn, Dr. Charles Stanley encourages you to see everything as coming from God, both the good and the so-called bad. The Bible tells us, "When times are good, be happy; but when times are bad, consider: God has made the one as well as the other" (Ecclesiastes 7:14). In the book of Job, after his series of calamities, his wife suggested he "curse God and die" (Job 2:9). Job simply responded, "You are talking like a foolish woman. Shall we accept good from God and not trouble?" (Job 2:10). We can learn from his faith and that of Solomon.

Life is, for sure, sometimes very tricky and complex on many levels, which can make our efforts toward loving ourselves a challenge at times. We may find that our bodies are weary but being driven, as we may be, we find it difficult to take time to ourselves or with God. He loves us so much; we should try to grasp that and work from that foundation. We develop the inner muscles of healthy self-love by living by the Spirit, as Paul exhorts, seeking God, even in the seemingly small matters. Don't doubt that God is in and cares about the minutest details of your day, including the color of the socks you chose today.

God's Word tells us, "There is now no condemnation for those who are in Christ Jesus" (Romans 8:1). This is an especially precious verse to me because I was prone to self-condemnation and flagellation due to the scapegoating I had received. In fact, when I first accepted Jesus into my heart on an altar call, I repeated this the following week in church because I thought I had not done it right. After that altar call, we were ushered into a room, where we who had come forward met with a counselor. The one I saw spoke with me and then quoted Romans 8:1. I had been listening to those negative tapes I spoke of earlier and had not accepted that Jesus had sealed the deal the first time I went forward. Voices of condemnation, whether from in our own minds or from another, do not come from God and do not fit us as His children, as Dr. Charles Stanley would say.

CHAPTER TEN

HEALTHY SELF-LOVE – PART 2

Self-talk can be another way of loving yourself and can be useful to counter voices of condemnation. In being positive out loud, you can hear yourself—or, more accurately, the little child inside can hear you—say good, loving things, and he or she is comforted.

When someone gives you a compliment, do you find it hard to take in? Healthy self-love involves learning to accept compliments and positive feedback from others, from God, even from yourself; you can literally say to yourself out loud, "Well done, [fill in your name here], well done," after you have completed a task to your or your boss's satisfaction. This is especially helpful for those of us who did not receive regular affirmation and encouragement from our parents when we were young. For those who feel very uncomfortable with praise, truly taking it in takes practice, practice, practice. If you experience a feeling of ill-ease upon receiving compliments, know that that feeling will fade in time as you work at allowing them in, recognizing that healing is a process, not an event.

We are all works in progress. We are all on a healing journey with Jesus. We are all learning how to love each other, ourselves, and God. "Seek first his kingdom and his righteousness" (Matthew 6:33). How it pleases Jesus when we first think of Him and His comforting presence in our daily lives—not only when things are good but especially when things go awry. We can count on His divine guidance. He will ultimately lead us only toward good (Romans 8:28), toward love, though it may not look like it at the time.

No one on the planet can do for you what Jesus can. The hymn "No One Ever Cared for Me Like Jesus" is one of my very favorites. It tells us, "No one else could take the sin and darkness from me." Hallelujah! Clearly, there is no one like the Lord! In seeking Jesus, He may direct you to His Word, which, when used and applied appropriately, provides comfort and peace to the born-again believer, even though there may be mystery and unanswered questions as well. Be forewarned, though, that before you open your Bible, you need to go to God and ask that He and He alone speak to you. The devil can twist and use scripture for his own purposes.

In the temptations of Jesus, the devil quoted scripture (Matthew 4:6). He is very tricky; we need to be extra careful. We are not only subject to temptation by Satan, but we also are fallible and prone to stumbling. Be patient and forgiving with yourself, if this is you today. Jesus also used scripture in His encounters with the devil. It is, therefore, so important to learn what is in the Bible—to study it, meditate upon it, and memorize it. Only then, when you are confronted with a temptation, can God's Word flow out of you and come to mind to help defeat the enemy, stopping him in his tracks. This is all part of healthy self-love.

We can even quote scripture out loud to send the devil packing. This practice is powerful! Verses like Philippians 1:6 and 1 John 4:4, mentioned earlier, are potent to fend off the enemy. Truth is, "All Scripture is God-breathed and is useful for teaching, rebuking, correcting and training in righteousness, so that the servant of God may be thoroughly equipped for every good work" (2 Timothy 3:16–17). Fact is as well that with our finite minds, we were not meant to understand it entirely, considering that it has an eternal quality to it. So don't worry if you cannot fully grasp the Word. Even still, someone once said, "We don't read the Bible; the Bible reads us!" He will use it to comfort us individually in our efforts to love ourselves; it's one big-energy book.

Pertaining to the scriptures, Christ, the subject of them, "is the same yesterday and today and forever" (Hebrews 13:8). Hallelujah again! He is not influenced by moods, the weather, or illness, nor does He need to grow in any area and "will neither slumber nor sleep" (Psalm 121:4). He is up and available to us at any time, day or night. Both the Word and He are completely trustworthy. (Incidentally, "hallelujah" is Hebrew for "we will praise the Lord." It is derived from the Hebrew verb, "hillel", "lu" is the second-person, masculine, plural suffix and "jah" is short for "Yahweh.")

When the devil drags us to our knees, though we can find it tough to even pray, we can trust that "the Spirit helps us in our weakness. We do not know what we ought to pray for, but the Spirit himself intercedes for us through wordless groans" (Romans 8:26). The Holy Spirit is working on our behalf, even when all the fight has gone out of us. As I said, we can trust God, even when all around us is trying to pull us away, including other people.

In learning to love ourselves, we must choose carefully those we allow into our inner circle. I personally have taken a stance against yelling. If someone begins to yell at me, I say, "If you do not lower your voice and regain control, I will leave"—difficult if it happens in my own home. That's why I only allow safe people into my refuge, my sacred space, my home.

We can trust God to give us words to speak and the courage to say them, just because we asked Him. He can also give us wisdom as to whom we should allow in our lives. Even the people in my life who are blood relatives need to prove themselves as safe people before I will have them in my inner circle. Two people from my family of origin are no longer in my life for this very reason.

While it's true that we were made to live and operate in community, it is ultimately God who provides people in our lives with whom we can share human intimacy. God is more acquainted with our needs than we are. We can rest in that fact—that He, being Jehovah Jireh, our provider, will tend to our needs as we look to Him to do so (Philippians 4:19). We exercise wisdom by going to Him for everything. Yet we can get stuck in our prized independence, using self-will and self-determination, resisting total dependence on God.

Indeed, society clings to and values independence. For instance, I like to do as much as I can for myself, like most anyone, and I can tend to feel a little slighted when anyone tries to take that from me. When I am at the grocery checkout line, and someone offers to help me unload my basket, I politely say, "No, thanks, I'd rather do it myself." While I know folks mean well, there is something called "wheelchair etiquette." It respects whatever independence the disabled one has left. No matter how tempting it may be to offer help, wheelchair etiquette says that one should withhold offers to help a person with a disability. Though well-intentioned, such an offer actually accentuates and highlights the disability. A disabled person is typically very adept at asking for help when he or she needs it. I'm reminded of something I learned in my training to be a therapist: "Never do for the client what they can do for themselves."

Maybe you can think of times when you were unhappy with someone limiting or cutting in on your independence. Sometimes, however, our bent toward independence and our love of it can be fueled by the unhealthy pride to which I referred earlier—pride that keeps us from reaching out.

My father used to be such a man. He was taken to the hospital only when his dementia got to the point where he didn't recognize his own house. Even then, he refused to believe anything was wrong or that he needed help. Thankfully, he grew out of that attitude with the help of God. In the last few years before his death, Dad was very adept at accepting and receiving the help he knew he needed. It was a marvelous thing to witness the transformation from staunch independence to interdependence that God wrought in his heart.

Friends and relatives may see that the independent, prideful one needs additional help, but this person staunchly presses on, ignoring the warning signs and the extra assistance that is often so readily available in our Western world.

> There is a time for everything, a season for every activity under
> the heavens. (Ecclesiastes 3:1)

There's a time for doing for ourselves and a time for reaching out. While it's true that we need to seek God first in all we do, sometimes we can come to end of ourselves, even with the support of friends and loved ones. We can arrive at a sense that there is more going on inside of us, stuff making us tick, that makes life more challenging—stuff we may have noticed and perhaps wondered about.

> For lack of guidance a nation falls, but victory is won through many advisers. (Proverbs 11:14)

> For by wise counsel you will wage your own war, and in a multitude of counselors there is safety. (Proverbs 24:6 NKJV)

I encourage you to keep an open mind on the delicate topic of counseling, or psychotherapy. What I have to say may surprise you.

While I've said that we are to go to God first, that doesn't mean we are to go to God *only*. God provides trained helpers in this difficult life who are ready and willing to assist us along our journey so that it can turn out to be that "full life" of which God spoke (John 10:10). Sometimes, we need to love ourselves enough to give ourselves this extra bit of support to get ourselves back on track, move forward, and find wholeness.

Coming up, we will explore more on this vital subject.

CHAPTER ELEVEN

GOD FIRST, NOT
ONLY—PART 1

You may feel that you are functioning fine—you hold down a job and have good friends and close relatives. Particularly if you were raised in a godly, loving environment with spiritually and emotionally healthy parents, who helped you from a young age to work through your pain as it came up, know that God has truly blessed you with a strong foundation, and it's appropriate to have healthy pride in that.

However, given that we are all fallen in nature, every one of our parents raised us with some degree of dysfunction. Though you may have had less dysfunction than some, realize that counseling is not just for the severely broken. It is for anyone willing to face their demons, to discover, unpack, and uncover hurt that may have become hidden in their subconscious minds. This type of hurt can result from residual emotion from a painful event, either in childhood or in youth, such as the death of a pet or a person or other difficult happening that was not fully resolved with the help of one's parents or guardians. It doesn't always result from early childhood trauma, such as abuse of any kind, including neglect, or from other emotional trauma, such as divorce, or losses of any kind, including loss of mobility.

Granted, counseling is a contrived, artificial relationship, perhaps with an unnatural feel to it, especially at first. The clinician is paid, and the counseling is solely and exclusively for the purpose of healing for the client. However, given this concentration on clients and their issues, it can be pivotal and like no other human relationship. Talking about and working through deep, messy emotions can be like connecting the dots. Over a period of weeks, one begins to see more of the full picture come into view. Not only the past but the future can start to take more shape, coming in with more clarity and more hope.

In connecting the dots, we can gain new insights into our own behavior and that of others in ways and at a depth we had previously not seen. Miracle work/ deep heart surgery can be accomplished through healthy counseling. I use the adjective *healthy* because there are also severely dysfunctional, even perverted therapists working in the field. As I mentioned, my first helping professional was such a man.

I bolted from his office and never went back. He demolished my trust in helping professionals; it wasn't until years later that I again sought professional help. But I did, and as it turned out, I was so grateful I had done so. Having a biochemical imbalance in one's brain and being without an appropriate clinician in one's life is fuel for disaster.

In the process of counseling or psychotherapy, as safety is established and trust is built between the therapist and the client, emotions deeply buried in the subconscious begin to surface in the client in order to be revisited, re-felt, and ultimately healed. Unfortunately, the only way to heal such emotions is by applying oneself and persevering through them. Here, the old adage, "No pain, no gain," holds true.

Being the family scapegoat, I did not know what safety in a relationship was. I had no special aunt or other relative who reached out to me while I encountered the abuse. Maybe you are a person who does not know safety, as all your earliest encounters were with severely dysfunctional people. "Safety" in counseling, could be described as a feeling of ease, where one can relax and share whatever one wishes. It is this element, coupled with the trust that accompanies it, that can be so very healing in the therapeutic setting.

Those who have been dealt cards, through no fault of their own, that involved more dysfunction, even early childhood trauma, suffer from a distinct disadvantage, as that unresolved emotion can end up running them. Folks who are prone to angry responses or who have hair-trigger tempers, for instance, may suffer from unresolved emotion piggybacking on everyday responses to stressful situations. I know someone who very rarely gets angry and faces stress that comes up as a part of life. She's able to, as the song says, "Keep on the sunny side" and disregard negativity. Mind you, she has a strong faith in Jesus and has had years of her own therapy, despite her own very dysfunctional start. Here are a few lyrics from her theme song (from the soundtrack of *O Brother, Where Art Thou?*):

> Well, there's a dark and a troubled side to life
> There's a bright and sunny side too …
> Keep on the sunny side …
> And let us trust in our Savior always
> He'll keep us, every one, in His care.

This person feels that her life has been deepened and enriched, that she is living that full life that her Savior promised, as a result of pursuing individual counseling.

We don't need to live our lives in misery, depression, despair, or even anxiety; there are answers, and help is available. Dr. Charles Stanley speaks of some who live "settled-for lives," in which they accept less than all God intended for them. Let that not be us.

Reality is cruel, in that pain that we incurred as children, through no fault of our own, is something for which we are ultimately responsible. We can learn to face wounds put there by a family member when we were just a victim, and we can learn new ways of functioning, foregoing old, ingrained, negative patterns. Realize this: if you encountered childhood abuse of any kind, again, I'm so sorry you went through that; you need to know, however, that you actually feed into and give the perpetrator(s) energy and victory if you decide not to unpack and work through the pain in counseling. (Generally speaking, it's not a good idea to seek resolution for hurt incurred in childhood directly from the perpetrator. Sometimes, that person may, in fact, cause further injury. Author Joyce Meyer did it when she confronted her father about the incest he inflicted on her, but she is the exception, rather than the rule.)

We don't choose our starts, but we do have more control over how we handle them than we might think. I believe, however, that even if you had a strong beginning, life can get complex, become so painful, where spiritual warfare can be so intense that you may one day find yourself needing additional help. Sometimes, we can get stuck in our pain and/or grief and are unable to move forward. In such cases, counseling may become a necessity.

Acknowledging your need of a two-person approach involving professional input and guidance for a complicated, messy, and troubling issue can be an expression of strength and wisdom. Counseling can become addictive, though, especially if therapists foster a dependence in the clients on the clinicians themselves. Know that healthy therapists encourage clients to rely on their own personal strengths and—if the clinicians are godly ones—ultimately, on God.

CHAPTER TWELVE

GOD FIRST, NOT
ONLY—PART 2

Studying scripture is another way we can find tremendous healing. Joyce Meyer can can attest to that; in fact, she quit her full-time job so that she could spend a year studying the Word to prepare for what she felt called to—a world-wide ministry. She found such strength, courage, and healing in the Bible that she was able to then take the necessary steps to embark on that ministry. Mind you, she had her faithful husband—himself a strong believer— by her side all along the way. Nonetheless, she fought for her life.

We too need to fight for our relationships. When there is a commitment to work things through when the going gets tough, that relationship or friendship can be extremely healing and fulfilling. Sometimes, however, boundaries are lax, are not respected, or are nonexistent, and trouble flares up. At this point, both parties have the choice to hang in there and do the work necessary to salvage the friendship or relationship, or to mutually decide to call it quits and part company. Sometimes, one party is not willing or able to move forward, and a stalemate occurs. Remember that trouble is inevitable. Though we wish and hope that things will go smoothly, life can go very awry, and we can find ourselves facing deep roadblocks to communication. If this is the case with you—if your partner is unable to move forward and/or refuses counseling— the best thing you can do is go into therapy yourself. Do it for yourself. The changes that your partner will see in you may later influence him or her to get his or her own help.

Life and health are both fragile. Given the complexity of emotions and the reality of the difficult nature of human relationships and dysfunctional families, we can find ourselves exhausted and on a dead-end road, with no answers and little hope coming in. In such cases, it's important not to give up. There is help; a fresh perspective can make all the difference. A counseling professional can help bring a fresh, objective view into our pain, if we are willing to do the work. Sometimes, we can be so immersed in our anguish that we cannot see the forest for the trees. I say it again: don't give up. Counseling can be so powerful that it can even act to rebuild our emotional foundations.

Especially with regard to depression, bipolar disorder, obsessive compulsive disorder or schizophrenia, medication is necessary. Mental illnesses are often biochemical imbalances. It is not a sign of weakness or addiction to take psychiatric medication. When medication is first introduced, many will balk at it, thinking that by taking it, their own willpower or their faith is somehow failing them. This is how I responded when antidepressants were first offered to me. However, nothing could have been further from the truth. Just as a person with type 1 diabetes needs insulin to function (indeed, to live), medication is essential to adjust the brain chemistry of a person with a particular mental illness. Psychiatric medication makes a world of difference and can return the person's mind, which was lost in deep despair, for example, to health and functioning again. Antidepressants, for instance, bring emotions to the point where people can actually get in touch with their feelings and thus be enabled to begin the work of counseling.

In many cases, medication is a prerequisite to proceeding effectively with counseling. Often, in the treatment of illnesses of the mind, like major depression or anxiety disorders, counseling and medication work hand in hand.

Engaging in counseling and learning to accept psychiatric medication are both processes, not events. One needs to commit to about ten to twelve sessions of steady, weekly counseling before changes may be detected. As well, antidepressants, for instance, take about two weeks to have full effect. Once a person agrees to take medication and has overcome that first hurdle, there still may be a lengthy struggle. Sufferers may be on medication for a while and then stop taking it because they feel better, only to plummet again. This cycle is normal. Remember that it takes time, years perhaps, as was the case with me, to adjust to the meds. It also takes a good psychiatrist to appropriately prescribe and educate the sufferer regarding the meds. A fellow more-experienced sufferer who is willing to explain the meds to the one who is new to them also can help that person come to a clear acceptance of the pills, if they are, in fact, what the doctor ordered.

What are the signs that you might need help? Some clear indications that it's wise to seek professional counsel are when your problems are wearing out your friends and family, and/or if symptoms, such as anxiety and/or depression, are persistent and relentless. Therapists are trained at listening and helping you work through the therapeutic process, but only psychiatrists are specialists in psychiatric medication and should be the ones prescribing it. Family physicians can prescribe, but they do not have the expertise and specific knowledge of psychiatric medication that a psychiatrist does. If a biochemical intervention is necessary or the need arises for a medication adjustment, therapists and general practitioners (GPs) do not have the expertise to properly prescribe and treat in such cases. In other words, should a client become psychotic, the GP would not know what to do. (*Psychosis* occurs when the sufferer is not aware that he or she is out of touch with external reality. Visual and/or auditory hallucinations can accompany this condition—symptoms that can be extremely distracting and tormenting to the sufferer.) This is the reason why anyone with a mental illness needs a competent psychiatrist.

I do know of folks with mental disorders who originally had a psychiatrist, but that doctor retired or moved away, so the GP then prescribed the medication. This is fine in the short term.

The wide variety of psychiatric medications available range from antidepressants, to antianxiety meds, to antipsychotics. Antianxiety meds are minor tranquilizers. Antipsychotics, generally known as major tranquilizers or neuroleptics, treat someone in acute psychosis, as the name suggests. A form of psychosis known as *delusions* is a severe symptom of major mental illnesses, like bipolar disorder, depression, and schizophrenia. The movie *A Beautiful Mind* offers an understanding about this devastating symptom. With this symptom, sufferers often find themselves catapulted into a strange and elaborate world, which can be exciting but also terrifying. Auditory hallucinations in the form of "voices" are common here as well. The only cure for delusions—indeed, for all psychoses—is a competent psychiatrist, along with the sufferer's acceptance of the treatment. I was suffering from delusions for a full nine months at the time of my jump; prior to it, I had gone to the emergency rooms of various hospitals over sixty times. The voices tormented me and the elaborate world that I lived in caused me to believe that it was my fault I was not getting better. I also seriously feared homelessness, as I was unable to look after my apartment. It was these things as well as the inactivity of professionals, as I've said, that caused me to do what I did.

Friends and relatives may find themselves confessing that they are not properly equipped to deal with the sufferer's situation. They may not know what to say or do. (I tackle this later in the book.) If you suspect your friend or relative is not in touch with reality, he or she needs specific psychiatric and pharmaceutical help from a licensed psychiatrist.

Back to counseling, psychotherapists are clinicians who are trained to listen for feelings and—hopefully, if they are good at what they do—give clients and the clients' issues their full and undivided attention and effort. A good therapist will not tell clients what to do but will empower and speak with the clients to help them decide the next step for themselves.

In the case of a sudden trauma, where sufferers are thrown off balance and stability is temporarily displaced, getting additional help in the form of counseling may provide enough strength so that, over time, they can find healing, stability can return, and they can pick themselves up and go on. Again, a biochemical component may be involved in such cases, but that determination should be left to a psychiatrist, a referral to whom one can get from one's family doctor.

CHAPTER THIRTEEN

NOT A SIGN OF
WEAKNESS—PART 1

The topic of counseling is such an incredibly rich one that I need to say more regarding it; do stay with me. As you ponder my words, it might bring a struggling friend to mind, or possibly, you may find yourself relating to what I have to say.

Adults who were abused as children may believe the lie that there is no one safe in the entire world. Their lives can be characterized by isolation, fear, and mistrust. I have a relative for whom this is the case. If they accept this lie as truth, they may be lost in a maze of falsehoods that could stay with them until their dying day.

Sometimes, these folks can also get caught up in another series of lies—that the hurt they experienced was their fault, that somehow they deserved it, that it was right for them. Abuse is never the victim's fault; it stems from a vicious choice made by the perpetrator. False guilt needs to be named and released so the victim can feel empowerment and relief.

It is never a sign of weakness to embrace the need for help. Indeed, it can indicate that you care enough about yourself and have enough insight to realize when you are overwhelmed to the point of needing trained help.

Regarding counselors and therapists, though, be forewarned. Just because someone has a degree in psychology or counseling and impressive credentials does not make that person a good fit for you. You need to shop for someone with whom you "click" or with whom you can be yourself and feel relaxed. If you make the decision to seek professional help, make appointments with various clinicians with whom you think you might like to work, and carefully and prayerfully consider who is best for you after experiencing each one. Granted, this is a lot of work, but the therapist holds a great deal of power. Be sure to find one who will not misuse it.

If you are considering counseling, my sincere hope is that you will choose a praying, godly therapist—*praying* because tremendous support can come through the righteous prayers of a solid Christian, and *godly* because it's so helpful to have the Holy Spirit as the third person in the sessions. Clinicians who seek their guidance from God can be true conduits of His divine love. Such professionals can act as "Jesus with skin on 'im."

Maybe you've heard the story about a little boy being tucked in bed for the night. His mother kissed him on the forehead, shut out the light, closed the door, and went downstairs to clean up the kitchen. Soon thereafter, she heard her son calling down to her, saying that he wanted her to come up because he was afraid of the dark. She called to him from the kitchen, telling him that he could simply pray, that Jesus was right there with him. His response was, "Yeah, but I want Jesus with skin on 'im!" Sometimes, we all need a godly human representative of the Savior to guide and comfort us. There is nothing wrong with and no shame in that.

We may require the additional trained support of a godly counselor, especially if we have trust issues. If we were abused or not allowed to have full dependence on our parents in the formative years, as examples, this can result in such issues. What are some signs that you may have these? You suffer from a lack of closeness with others because of mistrust; the lack of trust is causing problems in your relationship with your partner; you have volatile relationships (either one after the other or all at one time). As a result, family-of-origin counseling may be needed; it is as the name suggests—where feelings for each member of the client's family of origin come up to be healed. This process can be extremely terrifying, requiring all one has inside, plus God's strength, to tackle it, depending, of course, on the degree of dysfunctionality involved. The process can be so frightening because of the depth of pain and fear that can be uncovered, especially for those who were badly abused as children. In such cases, that one needs to grieve a lost childhood.

Healthy self-love may mean seeking to lessen the emotional baggage that we carry. My goal is to enter heaven with as little unresolved emotion as possible. I truly believe that it could result, in some way, in my not enjoying heaven to the greatest and fullest extent possible. Sometimes we can wonder why God allowed us to suffer as we did, whether it was wounding from our childhoods or other deep pain. Joni Eareckson Tada admits that her quadriplegia taught her that she needs God desperately; indeed, we all do.

Counseling also can show us how to get in touch with and express emotions in a healthy way. Because of my troubled upbringing, I have sought counseling for more than thirty years, mainly from Christian professionals, and mainly because of the myriad layers of hurt that have come up over the years. Early childhood abuse is composed of layers upon layers of hurt, much like the layers of an onion. A person can work in therapy on a specific issue, only to find that, years later, he or she needs to revisit that very same issue. (Granted, now, I only see my therapist on an as-needed basis for tune-up maintenance, maybe once a month or every six weeks.)

You can learn to identify and unlearn wrong ways of handling your feelings, substituting better ones in their place. Psychotherapy can help you identify and recognize triggers or areas of emotional sensitivity. For instance, someone might have a particular sensitivity toward being abandoned if that person's parent left when the person was a child. Since my father left when I was four, I have found that if a loved one pulls back even slightly, I can be prone to interpret that action as abandonment, even when it is nothing of the sort.

With triggering, emotion previously repressed can be ignited by a word or circumstance and cause the emotional response to be blown way out of proportion. It should be noted here that triggering may go on for a person's entire life, depending on the degree of hurt and abuse that he or she endured.

Repression is an unconscious mechanism that typically happens when, for instance, a child experiences strong, difficult emotions, such as rage, fear, or guilt. If the child's parents or guardians do not help the little one process such feelings, the child may repress them into the subconscious.

I witnessed violence in my home when I was four. My parents were unable to help me process what happened, so deep guilt, anger, rage, and fear became deeply embedded in my personality. Those feelings, particularly fear, still challenge me today as an adult. It has been through healthy therapy that I have found deep healing, although, again, not total eradication of triggers.

Repression can also occur with adults who go through severe emotional trauma. These repressed feelings hide but can be accessed and healed later in life when the person chooses to go beneath the surface. They might do this by seeking the help of friends or family, but healthy counseling provides concentrated attention on the pain. It's a two-person approach to heavy, intricate issues, with no expectation that you give back, as in a friendship. In counseling, it is your time for your individual healing, with no need for attention to or caring for the other individual, the professional. This is particularly helpful for folks who, as children, were faced with caregiving for their struggling parents. *Parentification* has also been called "emotional incest," as it carries that much pain and wounding with it. Parentification occurs when parents look to their child to support them, often divulging their very adult problems to their child, who cannot possibly handle this role; despite this, the child is then forced into the position of attempting to help. Hence, the child, in essence, becomes the parent of the parent, and roles are reversed. For those who did not experience healthy parenting but instead had parents they had to nurture and support as children, the therapeutic setting, with its one-sided nature, can be especially freeing and liberating.

CHAPTER FOURTEEN

NOT A SIGN OF
WEAKNESS—PART 2

$\mathcal{M}$y aim is to educate you regarding counseling or psychotherapy as much as I can, hence it's lengthy discussion.

A phenomenon in counseling called *transference* occurs when the subconscious feelings for the parent who is the same gender as the counselor interact within the therapy itself. This process requires skillful handling by a trained therapist to help the client acknowledge, experience, and finally express these potentially painful, previously repressed emotions. These emotions, in general, can contribute to physical health problems, even to suicidal ideation.

When one experiences the painful state of being suicidal, one needs to talk so that the power of the deep emotions that are behind the suicidal thoughts can be lessened and brought under control. Assistance can come from many sources; certainly, friends and family can help here too, but I must stress again, especially if suicidal ideation is prolonged and intense, hospitalization is necessary. The suicidal person needs to be kept physically safe and prevented from acting on those most powerful feelings.

In the movie *Pilgrim's Progress: Journey to Heaven* (a very favorite of mine, based on the book by John Bunyan), the protagonist, Christian, finds himself in the Doubting Castle of Giant Despair. The giant's wife suggests to the giant that he give Christian and his companion means to end their lives—a knife, some medication, a noose. Though the exhausted and despairing Christian is tempted by this, he inevitably, with a strong arm, pushes the means away.

Suicidal ideation can run so deep and be so complex that the sufferer requires the expertise of skilled mental health professionals—psychiatric nurses and a competent psychiatrist, who can determine if there is a biological, physical component to the depression, something that generally goes hand in hand with suicidal thoughts.

In the case of depression, electro-convulsive therapy, or ECT, can be so helpful. Now, don't be turned off by my mentioning this. It is much more effective and humane than it was in its early years of use. In days gone by, there was permanent memory loss as a result of the treatment. Nowadays, there is some memory loss associated with ECT, but the memory returns over time. It is such a powerful treatment that it can alleviate the symptoms of depression, though psychiatric professionals are not sure how it works.

Suicidal ideation can be brought on as abuse in childhood is triggered or even uncovered in therapy. That's precisely why the sufferer needs a very skilled, compassionate therapist at the helm of the therapeutic process.

It strikes me that receiving counseling is called *getting help* because that's purely what it is—getting help with complex, difficult, painful, and powerful emotions. Other reasons to pursue counseling are that it assists in gaining control and mastery over feelings so that clients don't behave reactively to situations; in addition, clients gain insight into their emotional makeup, creating profound and precious self-awareness, as well as into their individual emotional vulnerabilities, figuring out how they tick.

Certainly, when counselors are in counseling themselves, it helps them to become better therapists, as professionals learn what it is to sit in the other seat. In coming to a deeper understanding of themselves as clinicians, they can avoid falling into personal emotional pitfalls, including burnout, and they can be more present and helpful to their clients. In addition to therapists seeking their own individual therapy, each counselor should undertake supervision from a trained supervisor in order to unpack and evaluate the best approach to specific problems that the therapist's clients present.

Counseling builds patient endurance; it has the potential to teach clients how to express painful and challenging emotions in a godly and safe way. For instance, anger ought to be expressed in a godly tone, with words and a voice that remain in control, not with flying-off-the-handle tempers, with screaming and hollering.

"In your anger, do not sin" (Ephesians 4:26).

"Outbursts of wrath" (Galatians 5:20 NKJV) are called "works of the flesh" (Galatians 5:19 NKJV) and, therefore, do not fit us as children of God. If you are a screamer, know that you need to learn to bring yourself into control, and get help to find a more peaceful way to express your anger. Those who were severely damaged in their childhoods may have a lengthy struggle not only in learning to express anger in a godly way, but to accept godly love and receive goodness from God—or perhaps from anyone. They may find it especially difficult to receive good things from others as well as in relationship with themselves. (You *are* in a relationship with yourself, you know—is it a good one?) Again, they may feel that is what is they deserve: nothing could be further from the truth. Every child who comes into this world deserves deep, consistent love expressed in godly behavior from their parents.

When children grow up in a dysfunctional, fear-laden environment, *fear-heartedness* can develop that can be profound and far-reaching. I'm speaking again as someone who's been there. This happens when children are riddled with overblown, irrational fears that can torment and linger into adulthood. As a child, I had fear of developing cancer. I also felt I had to go to the grocery store with my mom to help her pick the food because I feared being poisoned. As a teen, I developed a phobia for germs that still rears its ugly head on occasion (although to a much lesser degree).

If you are feeling especially vulnerable to such attacks from Satan, know that there is hope. I encourage you to write out and repeat daily affirmations for yourself—truths about your particular gifts and talents. You may need to work on this with someone who knows you well. I encourage you to make the effort to do this: remember, you are worth it, and more. Please know and accept that you are precious in God's sight and worthy of all His best. You are infinitely precious and eternally loved by the God of the universe. To embrace this and feel it as a reality, though, again, can be a lifelong struggle. It's important not to give up. Healing for self-esteem and self-image is slow, but it does occur with those who are open to and ready for it. Actively receive and embrace the good—and that may mean with expert, trained support, no matter how foreign or awkward it may feel. You also need to face and discard the bad, no matter how it got there.

> Submit yourselves, then, to God. Resist the devil, and he will flee from you. Come near to God and he will come near to you. (James 4:7–8a)

By engaging in godly psychotherapy, you are definitely drawing near to Him. Remember: it is not a sign of weakness to accept help in the form of counseling; it's an indication that you are willing to unpack and work through pain that has gotten into you by virtue of just living life. It shows that you embrace that you are a work in progress. (If you find that you absolutely cannot afford a Christian counselor, freedomsession.com offers an alternative to biblical counseling that is healing and helpful. There is also Celebrate Recovery, a Christ-centered twelve-step recovery program for those with hurt, pain, or addiction of any kind. Either of these can be done in your local church setting.)

CHAPTER FIFTEEN
FORGIVENESS

Though not easily done, when someone hurts us, we can forgive by a conscious act of our will. We can make the *decision* to forgive. Saying the words out loud—"I forgive _____"—can be so powerful.

But there is also a process of forgiveness that involves working through the hurt feelings, such as anger or disappointment. In choosing to speak openly and honestly about those feelings with someone we trust, and in turn, to let go of those feelings, we then can embrace a new perspective in the relationship with the person who hurt us. This, too, is tough to do. It is real work.

We can learn from the Bible about forgiveness; for example, take the model of Jesus and His incredible capacity to forgive. He said of those who put Him on the cross, who slowly and brutally murdered the innocent Savior, "Father, forgive them for they do not know what they are doing" (Luke 23:34). In addition, when Stephen was being stoned, he "fell on his knees and cried out, 'Lord, do not hold this sin against them'" (Acts 7:60). These examples provide biblical models of a conscious act of forgiveness.

Recall, however, the story of the Prodigal Son (see Luke 15:11–32). The son took his inheritance and squandered it. We can only imagine what the father felt when his son demanded his share and walked away with it. Rather than reject the son, however, he set to work on his wounded feelings, unpacking them and talking about them, perhaps with his wife or trusted friend, so that, upon the son's return, the father "was filled with compassion for him; he ran to his son, threw his arms around him and kissed him" (Luke 15:20). Though the scripture doesn't say it here, the father likely went through a process of forgiveness. By virtue of his response when his son returned, it's evident he had worked through feelings he had when he saw his son take the money and run. Perhaps there was rage or at least disappointment, perhaps discouragement, but none of these feelings surfaced when the son came back. The father in the story of the Prodigal Son, then, provides a model to us of the power of the process of forgiveness. This process, however, can take days, weeks, months, or years, depending on the individual and the situation involved.

Just as the father in the story of the Prodigal Son forgave his son, so Jesus forgives us. As long as we are in this flesh, we will sin. Being born again does not prevent us from doing so. It merely provides baseline forgiveness for our sin nature and direct access to the One who is forgiveness, time and again, when we do sin. If you have owned a particular sin in your life and addressed it by repenting of it, Jesus has forgiven you for it.

> For as high as the heavens are above the earth, so great is his love
> for those who fear him; as far as the east is from the west, so far
> has he removed our transgressions from us. (Psalm 103:11–12)

When someone throws a past and forgiven sin back in your face, that's ultimately the devil's work. If there is a person in your life who is doing this, be aware of the source of that behavior.

Because we all are prone to sin, however, we need to make the daily choice to repent of any known or hidden sin, receive God's forgiveness, and let the shame wash away. Again, this is a choice.

Thank God for His forgiveness! Corrie ten Boom, author and Holocaust survivor, has said that when we confess our sins, God casts them into the deepest ocean, gone forever. She says she cannot find a scripture for it, but she believes God then places a sign out there that reads, NO FISHING ALLOWED. Perhaps you feel you have done something unimaginable and unforgiveable.

Perhaps you feel you have done something so terrible that you cannot envision a forgiving Savior. Rest assured; He *is* a forgiving Savior.

Recall that Jesus says, "For if you forgive other people when they sin against you, your heavenly Father will also forgive you. But if you do not forgive others their sins, your Father will not forgive your sins" (Matthew 6:14–15). This is very strong language. I suspect He means also forgiving ourselves, especially if we feel guilt-ridden over something we have done. If He can forgive us, shouldn't we take the oh-so-difficult step to forgive ourselves? We all make mistakes; we need to acknowledge this, and see ourselves as Jesus sees us—forgiven and complete in Christ.

To not forgive ourselves is to not receive the gift of forgiveness that Jesus has lovingly offered and for which He paid such a high price to deliver. For those of us who were not modeled forgiveness, especially in our early years, offering it to ourselves can be like venturing into the unknown. We need to use the same courage to embrace the new experiences that come from Christ, as we did when we reached to Him at the time of our conversion.

I'm amazed that both the act and process of forgiveness are paramount and remain ongoing necessities in this world where Satan is prince (John 12:31). We are regularly bombarded with situations in which there is the need to forgive, from being cut off on the roadways, to being blamed for something that went wrong, to being the brunt of someone's bad day. It may sound laborious, but with each new victory at every level, we can gain more mastery and more insight into our own emotional makeup, as well as into God's. As we relate to ourselves and others with the forgiveness of God, we can gain understanding into the very nature of God, since forgiveness was so central to the message of Jesus. It is only through the strength of Jesus, though, that we are able to forgive on a daily basis.

Unforgiveness, whether in relationships with others, God, or self, is a very heavy burden that inevitably causes a profound weariness. It also results in more problems for and harm to the one who has not forgiven than for the party at whom the unforgiveness is directed. The unforgiving one can be wracked with bitterness and anger that weighs him or her down, whereas the unforgiven one carries on with his or her life likely without any regard for the situation. We need to surrender our relational pain to Christ; in return, He can give us His lightness in our spirits. He alone can give us "a garment of praise instead of a spirit of despair" (Isaiah 61:3).

Know that only God can clear all the spiritual garbage from us. "If we confess our sins, he is faithful and just and will forgive us our sins, and purify us from all unrighteousness" (1 John 1:9). Notice that the scripture says *all*, not *some*. Count on this; trust in this promise of God and walk in the liberty that forgiveness delivers.

CHAPTER SIXTEEN
MERCY

$\mathcal{M}$ercy is defined as compassion or leniency shown toward someone for whom it is within one's power to punish or harm. Consider the next couple of verses:

> Let not mercy and truth forsake you; bind them around your neck, write them on the tablet of your heart, and so find favor and high esteem in the sight of God and man. (Proverbs 3:3–4 NKJV)

We all want that: "high esteem" with God and others. Therefore, I urge you to be merciful and truthful in your dealings with God, others, and yourself. Are you merciful, when you really think about it? Sometimes, we can lash out at someone in anger or be hypercritical of ourselves. Don't just surge forward in your car and cut off someone who just cut you off or roll down your window to give an unkind hand gesture. Pray for that person, and pray for yourself to exhibit a more godly and merciful response. Be extra kind to yourself if you find yourself in a habitual sin of some kind, recognizing that such behavior is difficult to break.

Let's turn directly to Jesus:

> The Lord is gracious and full of compassion, slow to anger and great in mercy. The Lord is good to all, and His tender mercies are over all His works. (Psalm 145:8–9 NKJV)

Sometimes, the Lord can shower mercy upon us that we do not fully acknowledge or receive. How often have we run through our day, not taking note of the many blessings of mercy that He showers upon us—that person who held the door open for us, the one who let us into a long line of traffic, that one who picked up something we dropped when our hands were full. You get the picture. Rest assured that His mercy is working in our lives, even though we may not take notice of it.

When it comes our time to meet Jesus face-to-face, He will then uncover the many times He was merciful to us, and we didn't even know it. Certainly, what God has offered us with salvation—what Jesus died to spare us from— is something we will grasp fully only on our judgment days, when we can actually see for ourselves the spiritual realms—the realities of heaven and hell.

Here is more from Jesus, regarding mercy:

> While Jesus was having dinner at Matthew's house, many tax collectors and sinners came and ate with him and his disciples.
>
> When the Pharisees saw this, they asked his disciples, "Why does your teacher eat with tax collectors and sinners?"
>
> On hearing this, Jesus said, "It is not the healthy who need a doctor, but the sick.
>
> But go and learn what this means: 'I desire mercy, not sacrifice.' For I have not come to call the righteous, but sinners." (Matthew 9:10–13)

For those who are in relentless pain of one sort or another, "I desire mercy not sacrifice" could relate to suicide. The World Health Organization says that one person dies by suicide every forty seconds. Though this is, of course, a serious problem for people of all age groups, among youth it takes an especially enormous toll, due to the significant years of potential life lost. Suicide is said to be the second leading cause of death among young people aged between 15 and 29, after road injury, and among teenage girls aged 15 to 19 it was the second biggest killer after maternal conditions. In teenage boys, suicide ranked third behind road injury and interpersonal violence. The youth are our future.

If you fall in that age category, God calls you to extend mercy to yourself and not give in to what is the ultimate in self-sacrifice. With God's help, you can find a way out of your problems, without taking the irreversible step of suicide. Please don't become a statistic. Come out and be strong in Jesus. Change is possible; in fact, it is the only constant in life. Fernando Ortega sings, "All the days of my struggle, I will wait for my change. I will wait for my change to come" (see Job 14:14). Can you wait? As you wait, you are being merciful to yourself.

Another act of mercy toward yourself occurred when you received Jesus as Savior.

> At one time we too were foolish, disobedient, deceived and enslaved by all kinds of passions and pleasures. We lived in malice and envy, being hated and hating one another.
>
> But when the kindness and love of God our Savior appeared, he saved us, not because of righteous things we had done, but because of his mercy. (Titus 3:3–5)

We accepted His mercy. Jesus revealed His mercy by showering His grace upon us at the time of our conversion (Ephesians 2:8–9). He, in turn, calls us to "Be merciful, just as your Father is merciful" (Luke 6:36). Consider also, "Speak and act as those who are going to be judged by the law that gives freedom, because judgment without mercy will be shown to anyone who has not been merciful. Mercy triumphs over judgment" (James 2:12-13). In addition, "Blessed are the merciful, for they will be shown mercy" (Matthew 5:7). We can trust in His promise of mercy as we take seriously the call to express it ourselves. Did you recently snap at someone in a moment of frustration, not meaning to, but the words just came out? We are all guilty, at one time or another, of not taming our tongues, even when it is called for. Hence, we need to be merciful not only to others but in our dealings with ourselves. To be merciful to ourselves when we lash out verbally is to immediately forgive ourselves and seek the forgiveness of those involved, if necessary. James says this:

> Those who consider themselves religious and yet do not keep a tight rein on their tongues deceive themselves, and their religion is worthless. (James 1:26)

Pretty strong language! I often pray, "God, give me the words to speak and the courage to say them." God can help us speak in a way that is pleasing to Him; we can engage with others with mercy in mind.

To include mercy in our speech and, indeed, in our lives, we need to exercise and engage our faith. Faith is the bridge between the temporal and the eternal. Jesus accused his followers of "little faith" (Matthew 16:8; Luke 12:28) and "rebuked them for their lack of faith" (Mark 16:14). We, in our humanity, can give in to the flesh, forgoing faith. Joyce Meyer says that because of the flesh, we want to sleep more when it's time to get up in the morning, and when it's time to sleep, we want to stay up. She calls us to sheer discipline to overcome these temptations. I would add here, though, that we need to exercise mercy with ourselves when we slip up, recognizing that we are in a war.

To me, mercy is forgiveness and love tied inseparably together. When we forgive, we exercise mercy and express love at the same time. Relating again to suicide, I need to say here that it expresses hatred, rage, anger, despair, or sorrow, for example, in behavior and action. These emotions are all difficult, but their power can be diffused and dissipated in an emotionally safe environment, wherever you might find that.

The Lord created difficult emotions, and He has a purpose in allowing us to feel them. Facing them with support, if necessary, causes us to be less prone to act on them. And clinging to the promises of God gives us strength in our spirits to handle the deep emotions that pain us; promises like this one:

> "For I know the plans I have for you," declares the Lord, "plans to prosper you and not to harm you, plans to give you hope and a future." (Jeremiah 29:11)

There are several promises in this one verse. Did you catch them? Elsewhere in the Bible, in many of the psalms, it strikes me that the authors, purely by expressing their pain, were able to find freedom and some resolution. They were merciful in their attitudes toward themselves as they worked through difficult emotions, proving once again that God was faithful in His mercy in return, as the psalmists were given precious insight and relief.

In the following verses, David expresses how God was merciful to him:

> To you, O Lord, I called; to the Lord I cried for mercy … Hear, O Lord, and be merciful to me; O Lord, be my help.

> What is gained if I am silenced, if I go down to the pit? Will the dust praise you? Will it proclaim your faithfulness?

> You turned my wailing into dancing; you removed my sackcloth and clothed me with joy, that my heart may sing to you and not be silent.

> O Lord my God, I will give you thanks forever. (Psalm 30:8–12)

As David realized, it's helpful to write out our anguish. We may feel emotions intensely, but with a little help from a pen and a journal, we need not get stuck in the emotions. Internationally renowned priest and prolific author, respected professor and beloved pastor, the late Henri Nouwen suggested that we befriend our emotions, even the nasty ones.

"In wrath, remember mercy" (Habakkuk 3:2b). Habakkuk was praying to God at this time, but when I read this scripture some time ago, God turned it around for me and suggested that I, in my anger, needed to remember mercy. If we could allow mercy to reign in our hearts, how much smoother life would be: road rage, emotional outbursts, and biting, sarcastic comments would be all but eliminated.

Jesus seeks your mercy to accomplish His good purposes. Mercy begets mercy. Perhaps you have heard the saying, "What goes around, comes around." As we deliver mercy, it comes right back to us. When God spared my life with the jump, I found that God's mercy *to* me elicited mercy *in* me. I, in turn, was able to be merciful to those responsible for my wheelchair. All this took place over years, however, requiring patience and mercy with God and His process.

If we expect Jesus to be merciful with us, we need to be merciful in our dealings with others. You might remember the parable of the Unmerciful Servant. The servant was forgiven a debt but then refused to show "mercy on [his] … fellow servant" (Matthew 18:33). This angered the first servant's master, and he had the servant sent away to be tortured until he paid back all he owed. Jesus then relates mercy with forgiveness, saying, "This is how my heavenly father will treat each of you unless you forgive your brother from your heart" (Matthew 18:35). Strong language again!

Being merciful to yourself includes embracing that you are good—"God saw all that he had made, and it was very good" (Genesis 1:31)—and that God is good—"I am the good shepherd" (John 10:11)—no matter what the trial. Doubt may tempt you, especially in periods of deep grief, but let this come and go. Don't dwell on it. It is not from God. With the world currently in the midst of the long-lasting COVID-19 pandemic, I said to a number of friends that I believed God was calling us, as believers, not to doubt His power or His mercy—despite that fact that nothing seemed to be happening in terms of a vaccine, for instance—but to keep on trusting.

May we learn to be merciful with ourselves, with others, and with the incomprehensible, uniquely eternal God, remembering and keeping in mind that His ways are not ours (Isaiah 55:8-9).

CHAPTER SEVENTEEN

ON ACCEPTING—PART 1

*I*n her book *On Death and Dying,* Elisabeth Kubler-Ross lists five stages of grief as denial, anger, bargaining, depression, and acceptance. Accepting your losses—such as the death of someone close to you, mobility issues, relationship breakups, or loss of a job or friendship—is the final step as you work through difficult emotions, such as anger and depression. In this chapter, I will explore the importance of coming to grips with our reality, despite how difficult that may be to accomplish.

One way to help us do that is to embrace and accept the truth that life is difficult as an objective fact. Can we objectify life, separating it from ourselves and seeing it more clearly for what it is? It may be, then, a bit easier to accept and embrace this truth that inevitably sets us free (John 8:32).

Another truth is that God requires a great deal of us just to keep us on an even keel. As I've said, God called Adam to "painful toil" (Genesis 3:17b) as a result of his disobedience in the garden of Eden. Certainly, if we plow a field and leave it, weeds grow. Silver tarnishes if left to sit. Rust seems to just happen on our cars, and mold appears if food is kept even in the fridge for some time. Extra pounds just seem to creep on our bodies, and it is such a challenge to rid ourselves of that excess weight. There's a saying, "A rolling stone gathers no moss." We need to press on, keeping in step with the pace of life, making good choices with regard to our health and overall well-being on a consistent basis, even if it means facing one difficult thing after the next, as that can just be the very nature of life as it is in reality. Life takes perseverance and persistence. Oh, how we need the strength of Christ!

We are to be in this world but not of it. The world has a nasty habit of throwing spiritual dirt at us; it is then our responsibility to do the work to regularly and routinely give it to God and let Him cleanse. This is why He provides the Bible and the Holy Spirit, who can reside within us to guide, comfort, and strengthen, as well as other people, family, friends, and professionals with whom we can fellowship and work through our issues.

Jesus knows how hard things can get. He suggests that we face and accept our journey in daily chunks:

> Do not worry about tomorrow, for tomorrow will worry about itself. Each day has enough trouble of its own. (Matthew 6:34)

Did you notice yet another promise there about having "trouble" in our day? In this world full of hardship, we are all on a unique journey that is one of a kind.

ONLY ONE YOU

Imagine—there is and ever will be only one you in all eternity! Take a moment to ponder that fact. You are a complete and utter original who has a set of circumstances and reactions that are absolutely unique to you. You have a personality—including strengths, weaknesses, likes, and dislikes—that is entirely yours alone. Hurts in your life are also yours and are your responsibility, no matter how they got there. You cannot choose how you had your start, but you can choose how you will play the cards you've been dealt.

I say again: you have experienced circumstances with a unique set of reactions all your own, for which you are ultimately responsible. What an awesome task! What enormous loneliness! God gives us the Holy Spirit to live within us, to be in our very breath, to be that close, so we do not collapse from loneliness. And He has promised to "never leave [us] … nor forsake [us]" (Deuteronomy 31:6, 8; Joshua 1:5; Hebrews 13:5). Andy Stanley said that one of the greatest things he learned from his father, Dr. Charles Stanley, was that there are times when he had to stand alone, particularly as a leader. I think that in all our journeys in life, not only as leaders, God calls us at times to do just that: we may be led to take a stance against a group or a person who believes one thing when the truth is actually something else. This group or individual could even be from our own families. Or perhaps we need to take a stand for an underdog who is under great social pressure. Maybe we feel we need to join in a rally or protest against racial inequality, like those for George Floyd.

Because we each are on a completely individual journey for which we are responsible, I need to again comment on the topic of counseling or psychotherapy as a vehicle that can provide significant healing. There is so much to say, yet I feel I have barely expressed its great benefits.

Repressed emotions, those hidden in the subconscious, can sap energy in a big way. To finally face and find expression of these emotions—to find freedom from their grip—is to uncover a huge source of emotional power or energy that was previously held inside the reservoir of pain. Release of repressed emotions can happen elsewhere, but it's often the work done in counseling that brings a new quickness to one's step as well as a lightness to one's heart.

In addition, a godly therapist can invite the presence of Jesus into painful memories, bringing comfort and solace in the midst of anguish. The therapist can ask the client who is describing a horrific event or story from his or her past how it feels to envision Jesus coming into the room at the time the event occurred. This can elicit the expression of feelings that can both deepen the sufferer's faith and provide emotional and spiritual healing. With such a practice, the power of Jesus can touch even the most intimate and private of hurts.

Friends and family may be limited in how far they are able to walk alongside you, with regard to certain challenges you face, or perhaps you don't want to drag them unnecessarily into the mire of your deep pain. You may choose to seek a professional so that you can come to that final stage of accepting your truth and the life realities in which you find yourself.

In regard to the regular daily warfare that we all face, sometimes it's good to have multiple sources of support—for example, a caseworker, social worker or a spiritual director—other than your therapist. Such helpers can be emotional weightlifters. They wade through the deepest of waters within their clients' souls and expect those they help to speak at length and in detail about the often-tremendous challenges they face.

A journey through the "valley of the shadow of death" (Psalm 23:4 NKJV) can further bring up pain yet unresolved. I found that when I had anticipatory grief for my dying father, new levels of pain surfaced and needed attention. When something like this happens, it can make life that much more difficult and complicated.

Unresolved painful emotions can be like a clog in our spiritual drainpipe. Having easy access to people who can act as sounding boards on troubling issues and offer care and compassion may elude us or may even distract us from working at the depths that are really necessary. We may find healing in relationships outside the therapeutic forum, especially when healthy relationships are modeled in our family of origin; however, this is not the case for those whose families were more dysfunctional. Such people may finally choose to face themselves with the help of counseling. Deep pain from their past can act as fuel to motivate them to stay the often lengthy and arduous journey in therapy toward health and wholeness.

There is only one of you. Maybe you want to learn about yourself, even the parts you fear and/or find distasteful. Maybe you want to explore your emotional makeup, live life to the fullest, and experience all the highs and lows it has to offer. Counseling can help you to do all that and more.

Finding expression for long-repressed hurt emotions can lead to a more satisfying, productive, and peace-filled life. It provides strength and self-control to prevent us from having such things as fits of rage, which are listed as one of the "acts of the flesh" (Galatians 5:19–20) and a root of bitterness, both of which do not fit us as children of God.

> Get rid of all bitterness, rage and anger, brawling and slander, along with every form of malice. (Ephesians 4:31)

It strikes me that we need to do this in our relationships with ourselves as well. We can be bitter and angry toward ourselves for something we have done or a mistake we have made. The Word of God reads, "See to it that no one falls short of the grace of God and that no bitter root grows up to cause trouble and defile many" (Hebrews 12:15), referring not only to our relations with others but with ourselves. Bitterness is a natural part of deep grieving, though, so if you feel it, do not chastise yourself. Instead, let it come and go. It can come with deep pain, but it's not something with which you should linger. Let it work its way through you and out.

Finally, with regard to getting help, the client and the counselor both, to varying degrees, can receive so much from working together—the therapist can gain precious insights from engaging with the client. Quite frankly, it's wise to embrace all the healing we can get in this life because we are all in—I'll say it again--a spiritual war.

SPIRITUAL WARFARE

Spiritual warfare is truth; it is a daily reality. Robert Morgan, in his book *The Red Sea Rules*, writes that life is particularly difficult for Christians. We have an enemy.

Jesus is the final victor over Satan, and as believers, we have direct access to His power and strength through the Holy Spirit. It is through Him that we can find the courage to live this difficult life, which includes torment from the devil. We can empower and strengthen the Spirit within us through reading, studying, and meditating on the Bible. In her book *Seeking God: My Journey of Prayer and Praise*, Joni Eareckson Tada writes that God has drawn her closer to Him through her injury. Her wheelchair, she says, drives her to seek His Word.

Indeed, God uses tragedy and trauma to draw us to Him. If you are facing either at this time, dig into the Word, and you will find more of Him. God can speak directly to us through His Word. During my early years as a Christian, I began dating an unbeliever. I asked God about this, and my Bible opened to 1 Kings 11, where it speaks of Solomon being pulled away from God by his pagan wives (verse 4). After reading this, I immediately broke off that relationship.

As well, we can discover Jesus more by seeking His will in a dialogue of prayer. God instructs us as to how to come to Him:

> Do not be anxious about anything, but in every situation, by prayer and petition, with thanksgiving, present your requests to God.
>
> And the peace of God, which transcends all understanding, will guard your hearts and your minds in Christ Jesus. (Philippians 4:6–7)

When I lived in the institution, I read this particular piece of scripture; it dawned on me at that time that this was a formula. As I prayed with thanks, God promised to give me His peace. And I found that was so true! Fervent prayer not only fosters intimacy with the Great I Am, but it can also help us find wisdom and guidance, especially in our relationships, where the spiritual warfare is often at its most intense.

Listening to God is also important, as we give Him time and space to interact with us. Dr. Charles Stanley admits that his strength and courage comes because very early in his life as a Christian, he learned to listen to God.

Because life is difficult and spiritual warfare is a reality, thoughts of suicide and the act itself are sad and tragic parts of this life. Intense pain, whether prolonged agony through circumstances or illness, can drive us to the very end of ourselves. Your enemy and mine would use that state to torment and belittle us to the point where we may feel convinced that ending life is the best solution. The operative word here is *feel*. (I will speak more on feelings in the coming sections.)

Again, Satan uses the mind to influence the emotions with the seven deadly Ds—he seeks to **d**isappoint and then **d**iscourage. Then he tries to keep us in **d**espair long enough that it leads to **d**epression and a **d**esire to **d**ie, which he hopes will end in our **d**eath by our own hand. I understand if you've felt this way; I understand that you want out of your pain, but you *can* find the strength to go on. You'll need to accept the truth that there is a devil and that he wants you dead in order to rob those around you--indeed, the world--of what you would have contributed, had you pressed on. Spiritual warfare is truth that we need to accept but it is a reality you can win with Jesus Christ. Attitude is key, something I will discuss in the following chapter.

CHAPTER EIGHTEEN

ON ACCEPTING—PART 2

Accepting at my "core" that life is difficult is so crucial. By this, I mean developing appropriate attitudes. I used to believe that because I had suffered in my life, I had a right to expect that things should go my way. When I was newly-injured for instance, I cursed God because I had had a difficult childhood and now, had to spend the rest of my years in a wheelchair. In hindsight, I can say that I was wrong to think that way. As long as I am on this earth, I will encounter difficulty. Recall that Jesus promised it (John 16:33; Matthew 6:34). The key is attitude—what we do with whatever comes our way.

AN ATTITUDE OF GRATITUDE

Years ago, God led me to develop an attitude of gratitude. When I was new to the wheelchair, I languished in suicidal despair for about three years. What pulled me out of it was giving thanks, thanks for a wheelchair I could get around in and that I wasn't quadriplegic but had good use of my hands. Developing this as an overall attitude truly was the key to lifting me up. I now try to live my life by a scripture I have on a carving on the wall in my living room that reads, "In Everything Give Thanks" (1 Thessalonians 5:18 NKJV). The last part of this verse says, "for this is God's will for you in Christ Jesus."

You know, I heard a story of Satan taking someone on a tour of his lair. There, they saw a room full of his "seeds." The person asked Satan what this was, to which the devil responded, "Those are the seeds that could not be planted because of grateful hearts."

Recording artist Robin Mark sings a lyric taken from Isaiah 61:3: "Put on the garment of praise for the spirit of heaviness." Indeed, and as was the case with me, this can make all the difference!

Can you find things for which to give God thanks, even something small and seemingly insignificant? There is a song that says, "Count your blessings, name them one by one, and it will surprise you what the Lord hath done." Indeed, I have found that when I start doing this, God opens my heart to find more and more for which to give Him thanks.

There may be blessings that you do not consider. For example, consider the ability of your body to change position when you sleep. People with spinal cord injuries, such as Joni Eareckson Tada, have to be turned manually during the night and use strategically placed pillows to prevent pressure sores. "Count your blessings, name them one by one, and it will surprise you what the Lord hath done." Surely in making the time to do this, you will be amazed as to just how many there are.

As you develop this attitude of gratitude, good works can spring from it. Perhaps God is calling you to volunteer in your local nursing home, hospital, or long-term care facility. I now volunteer as a pastoral visitor at the home where Dad stayed. I saw that most of the staff there treated him well. I was grateful for this and wanted to give back. I also value seniors so very much. I believe they are untapped sources of wisdom and experience. I feel they are rarely given the respect and appreciation they deserve in our culture. (Of course, with the COVID-19 crisis, I have been restricted from going to the nursing home; however, I still pray for the residents.)

Take seriously the call to be with the "least of these" (Matthew 25:40). Hanging out with such folks will help build an attitude of gratitude as you witness, firsthand, a more disadvantaged one struggling to cope.

AN ATTITUDE OF PRAYER

In the Bible, the verse directly preceding, "In everything give thanks" is "pray continually" (1 Thessalonians 5:17). I believe this refers to an attitude of prayer. We are to keep our gaze on the Lord, reaching to Him at all times. I used to believe that I merely had to have Him in the forefront of my mind and be willing to pray about anything and everything at any time. I now realize that this scripture means exactly what it says--a daunting prospect? Ask God to give you words to speak to Him as you venture through your day, and trust that He will.

When I met Jesus at my conversion, I was so thrilled to have an inner person to whom I could go, who could be with me wherever I went and in whatever I did, thought, and felt. It was so freeing and liberating to know that the Creator, the God of the universe, had come to reside in me and that I can access Him always. This is especially precious to me because I did not have anyone encouraging me when I was young. He is truly "a friend who sticks closer than a brother" (Proverbs18:24), no matter what.

Today, I try to keep uppermost in my mind the knowledge of His comforting ever presence, regardless of whether I *feel* it or not. Feelings are fickle; they can change on a dime. The truth is that God will never leave us. We need to trust that as fact and move forward with our days on that basis, speaking to God as we go. This is what I mean by having an attitude of prayer. Be assured though, that the devil especially hates a Christian who is intimate with God on a daily basis; Satan will try to hinder your communication with the Lord, you can bet on this.

In the garden of Gethsemane, just prior to His crucifixion, Jesus expressed that He was "overwhelmed with sorrow to the point of death" (Matthew 26:38). He said this to his disciples, asking them to pray before He went to talk to His Father. Intercessory prayer was crucial, even at *Jesus's* point of great agony. How much more do we need it? Even He needed good people around Him. It is important to develop a healthy social network, and that includes worshipping in a Bible-believing community. There is great power in gathering together as believers. Remember, "Every good and perfect gift is from above" (James 1:17). God is ultimately the giver of all good things, including a good church and good, helpful people. If you have it and them around you, thank God. They are His gifts to you.

William Paul Young, in his book *The Shack*, cleverly reveals the oh-so-loving relationship between the Father, Son, and Spirit—one of laughter and free-flowing, unconditional love, not of clinginess, compulsion, or obligation. We must remember that when we approach God, instead of carrying with us false notions of who He is, we need to be able to experience Him for who He actually is: love—pure love—peace, and joy. We can pray about this as well. God will reveal Himself simply for the asking.

Maintaining an attitude of prayer, then, is so crucial; it develops that intimacy with God that He so longs to have with all His followers.

SUFFERING AS A CALLING

When trials come our way, we should embrace them as elements of a calling from God to share in His sufferings. Recall Peter's words:

> If you suffer for doing good and you endure it, this is commendable before God. To this you were called, because Christ suffered for you, leaving you an example, that you should follow in his steps. (1 Peter 2:20b–21)

We are called to suffering, and we are called to persevere. God wants you to come near to Him, drawing on His example at His cross to give you the strength to bear *your* cross.

Do you spend time complaining about your trials but taking little action, or do you immediately see the hand of God in situations to which He brings you? Seeing your suffering as a calling can help you dig your feet in and stand in the midst of it (Ephesians 6:13). It strikes me that you don't have to do anything but stand; that that is enough. You don't have to jump through hoops and perform for Jesus; just stand.

If something happened to you that was beyond your control, God wants to use it to call you to a deeper walk with Him. You might not have been able to control what happened to you, but you do have control over your response to the suffering. Embrace the attitude of seeing your trial as a calling from God today.

PUTTING PARENTS INTO PERSPECTIVE

To accept that life is difficult at the core, we need to accept our parents with their failings and weaknesses. This attitude can lead us to sort through our feelings for our parents. It means letting go of blame and taking responsibility for any hurt or distress within, regardless of how it got there. We can either gain control and mastery over our hurts and our emotions, or they will gain control and mastery over us.

We need to acknowledge that our parents tried their best. They likely did not set out to intentionally hurt us, but perhaps, as in the case of dysfunction, powerful emotions got out of control, and hurt was inadvertently passed down, as was the case with my mom and the scapegoating. Putting parents into perspective also means letting go of childlike expectations for perfection. We should take our eyes off our parents and place them on the only perfect one, Jesus Christ.

If you were abused as a child and have (or plan to have) children of your own, you are at risk of repeating the pattern of abuse if you don't break the abuse cycle. It is generally through good counseling that this cycle is shattered. It is true that strong and biblically solid spouses can support the hurting one who had the abuse in childhood to such an extent that counseling is not necessary. Such was the case with author Joyce Meyer and her husband, Dave. But these occasions are rare. If you have that rare spouse or significant other in your life who is willing to help you work through deep hurts, as well as provide for you, spiritually and emotionally, know that you have been very gifted indeed. For many, however, friends can provide in this way, but for some, that person will be a professional, as they are without someone in their lives with whom to work through the deepest, most challenging emotions. The therapeutic environment indeed offers a place where trust is built in safety, without the insecurity of having to measure up, as is the case in some friendships.

Friendships can be consistent and loving, even unconditionally loving at their best, but often we do put conditions on our relationships. We spend a long time dating to determine if someone fits the bill as a future spouse. We can choose to walk away from someone in our lives because he or she behaves in a way or says something of which we do not approve. I once said goodbye to a friend I'd had for over twenty years because I was frustrated that he was not growing in his faith. I then heard a sermon that outlined the scripture that said, to each man, God gives "a measure of faith" (Romans 12:3 NKJV). So I went back to my friend and apologized for judging him. With my newfound understanding, our friendship is now stronger than ever.

We *should*, however, put conditions on our relationships in order to keep ourselves safe. That's why proper boundaries are so important and necessary in regard to healthy human-to-human interaction. They can be taught by our parents or caregivers, but again, they can also be learned in a therapeutic environment. Engaging in a therapeutic relationship is work that can change your life, as long as you're willing to put the necessary energy into it.

Boundaries can help you learn to choose healthy friendships and relationships: once such are established, you can learn to give and receive the unconditional love that God models for us.

It is also true that embracing the truth of who we are helps us to grow stronger to face the war in which we all find ourselves. Don't take your gifts, talents, and abilities for granted. They were put there by God. Spiritual gifts that God gave you at the time of your conversion can be uncovered and identified with the help of certain courses, such as the Network Kit by Zondervan. You also have other gifts with which you were born. Maybe your parents recognized that you exhibited a musical talent, for instance, at an early age and encouraged you to practice an instrument; in hindsight, you may be thankful for that. Putting your parents in perspective and accepting that life is difficult at the core also involves gratitude for all the efforts and responsibilities your parents *did* embrace to promote your growth as an individual.

Parents cannot teach what they do not know. An unhealthy parent, from either a spiritual or an emotional standpoint—or both—cannot be expected to raise healthy, functioning, functional children. Yes, children from parents of other faiths or without faith can be what the world sees as high achievers as they grow to adulthood, but if they want to do anything of *eternal* value, they need to receive Jesus and work as unto Him (Colossians 3:23). All people have been given free will to accept or reject the help and love Christ freely offers, not only with regard to salvation but with respect to the spiritual undergirding, joy, peace, and strength that learning to walk in the Spirit provides. Certainly and again, we have these choices.

It seems that most people from my parents' generation were unable to process their own childhood hurts, perhaps mainly because it was frowned upon in their generation to seek emotional help. Back then, anyone seeing a psychiatrist or other helping professional could face rejection or ostracism. Today, it is much more widely accepted to receive professional help. When it's necessary to engage in this process of healing in order to accept our parents as they are and were, we are well on our way to accepting that, at the core, life is difficult.

CHAPTER NINETEEN

ON ACCEPTING—PART 3

FOR PARENTS

I have not raised children, so I have a limited perspective, but I understand that just as it's an awesome, sometimes lonely responsibility to care well for oneself, it is doubly so for parents who are responsible for their little people. In light of this, I'd like to offer a few words of encouragement, especially to parents.

If parents truly accept at their core that life is hard, they can spare their children from feeling the harshness of life, which will free them to joyously run and romp as children should. By seeking to resolve deep issues in a responsible way, parents can function as a buffer, protecting their children from the harsh reality of life. The more seriously parents embrace their individual processes of healing, the less likely they are to pass on hidden pain to the next generation.

Abuse is committed for a number of reasons. Unresolved hurt can trigger inappropriate, unhealthy responses. Unhealthy responses also may stem from unhealthy attitudes, such as an unconscious expectation that life ought to be something different than it is, that life ought to be easy or go their way. If there is even a shred of this belief in a person, rather than that one experiencing life as difficult, as should be expected, he or she can experience life as generally torturous and unmanageable, an attitude that can be passed on to the children.

The greatest things that parents can teach their children, aside from a knowledge and experience of Jesus, His salvation, and His Word, is the ability to be assertive, to acquire proper boundaries to keep themselves safe. Predators are real and exist in virtually every level of society. Teach your children to be on their guard against suspicious behavior, and help teenagers learn to guard themselves against such ruthless people, then and on into adulthood.

Parents need to fully embrace and understand their responsibilities as mother and father, not only on a physical level but emotionally and spiritually as well. Healthy parenting requires a certain degree of maturity and stability if children are to grow and thrive. If these are not present, their children's world can be openly exposed to emotional pain that can plunge the children into sadness, anxiety, or even depression. In time, as these children become adults, they may feel ill-equipped to handle life's storms. They may be unable to embrace that life is difficult at a deep level as they themselves grow, as that was not modeled for them.

Parents, in particular, need to take their roles seriously and do the hard work to care well for themselves, first of all, because they are no good to their children without replenishing their own supply of energy. Each parent should feed off of Jesus, the bread of life. Going to the Word and spending time alone, as well as together, in communication and dialogue with Jesus are particularly essential daily practices for parents.

Parents also need to be aware that they are being watched very carefully. They are models. A child is like a sponge, absorbing all that is within his or her environment. If a parent is noticeably down, the child may try to cheer up the parent. If that parent takes a turn for the worse and then, sadly, makes the irreversible decision to attempt suicide, this can send the message to the children that when life is tough, it's okay to give up. Not only that, but children can become tormented by blaming themselves, thinking that they should or could have prevented it somehow. And it can lead to a greater likelihood or temptation for such children, when they are grown, to think of and, indeed, commit suicide.

Leading by example is the most powerful way to teach and take responsibility for your children. Action speaks louder than words, as the old adage says. If you are a parent, I encourage you to allow your children to know about the struggles you face—not to lean on your children for support, mind you, but to allow them to see you and God in action as you pray and work to resolve a particular issue in a godly way. As the children witness your dependence on God and interdependence with each other as a couple in a world where real problems exist, they can learn appropriate coping skills as they grow. This can provide a powerful model for the children as to how to deal with real troubles in life in a godly fashion.

Parents can be particularly vulnerable to discouragement and despair because of the relentless needs that children place on them. But with God's strength, drawing from the courage Jesus showed at Gethsemane and on the cross, parents can endure.

If you find yourself giving in to discouragement or despair as a parent, reach out to find healing. Help is available. It takes a brave man or woman to identify that there is a problem and take the steps to get the appropriate help. If you, as a parent are, feeling so down that you have contemplated suicide, know that it leaves a toxic trail of guilt for those left behind, especially for your children. Please try to go on, if only for their sakes. What a strong and wonderful heritage you will leave behind, not only for them but for your world to witness, if you accept yourself and life as it is, enduring to the very end, until God takes you home in His time and in His way.

ON PARENTIFICATION

I wish here to approach the topic of *parentification* in more depth. As a reminder, parentification happens when the parent looks directly to the child for adult support, and roles are reversed.

If a parent does share his or her adult problems with the children in order to gain support from them, that parent is actually stealing precious energy from them that the children need to grow healthily. With parentification, children will be faced with enormous pressure to support the parent, as they need that adult for their very survival. Children will end up straining and overextending themselves, and can become hypervigilant, excessively looking to solve problems in general.

Young children do not need their parents to be their friends; they need *parenting* parents who fully embrace all that parenthood entails. Children need firm but kind discipline that is consistent.

Parentification robs children of the innocence and carefree nature of a healthy childhood; indeed, it robs them of their childhood. In essence, it forces them to grow up way too fast. Such children tend to develop a sense of overresponsibility, taking on more than what is healthy for them. They can become tormented and obsessed with their parents' well-being and blame themselves when their parents are unhappy. And parentification can leave children with a false or exaggerated sense of power and self-importance, as those children believe they are somehow bigger and stronger than they actually are—bigger and stronger than their own parent(s). If this exaggerated sense of power is not checked, it can manifest itself as the child grows in ways that are not only unhealthy but painful, not only for the one exhibiting this behavior but for those around this person as well.

You may feel abandoned, spiritually and emotionally, as a parent. You may feel alone when raising your children, or perhaps you felt alone when you were a child. You may have a hard time coping in that aloneness. I caution you again not to lean on your young children. They do not need to strain under the weight of adult problems with which their immature, fragile spirits are ill-equipped to cope. Just as we, as adults, with our finite minds, cannot tolerate knowing the ways of God and the eternal reasons for what He does (Isaiah 55:8–9), so young children's minds need to be protected from burdens that are beyond their capacity to healthily embrace.

Though my mom made this mistake, she says that it was behavior she now regrets.

CHAPTER TWENTY
ON FEELINGS

It is important to try not to behave reactively on our feelings. By that, I mean not flying off the handle in a labile way when something goes wrong. As a reminder, we either can learn to master and control our emotions, or they will master and control us. The really high feelings, like elation, or the really low ones, like despair, come and go. Anne Graham Lotz, daughter of the late Billy Graham, says that she went through a dark period in her life when she actually felt abandoned by God. She also says, however, that she didn't put her trust in her feelings but in her faith in God.

Only Jesus is unchangeable, "the same yesterday and today and forever" (Hebrews 13:8). He is the rock and the only person on whom we are to stand. Again, I've lived some of my adult life with only Jesus available for me, in terms of daily contact, aside from my attendants. Jesus proved to be my refuge. He is our fortress—and I used *our* because it's in community that we triumph. Strength can be granted to us as we interact with members and leaders of our churches. The Holy Spirit guides, comforts, and communicates through the fellowship and worship. This is precisely why we should find a good Bible-believing church. Paul said, "Let us … not give up meeting together, as some are in the habit of doing, but let us encourage one another" (Hebrews 10:24a–25). It's so important to have a sense of belonging and inclusion into the family of God. We can speak with and get some strength from nonbelievers as well, but the Holy Spirit will be altogether lacking in the conversation. Be reminded that we need to make our relationship with Jesus our number-one priority. In my experience, it is in dialogue with God, in prayer and journaling, and by studying His Word that I can glean deep spiritual support.

Remember as well that with God, you are never alone (Deuteronomy 31:6, 8; Joshua 1:5). If you are born again, even though you may not feel the Holy Spirit, He is with you. He is there, regardless of what your feelings may be telling you, as Anne Graham Lotz discovered.

As you struggle with deep need, feed your spirit through fasting. As you do this, you will notice God supplying strength for you to face those difficulties. Fasting food is a wonderful practice that I have done for more than twenty-five years. If you are diabetic and need to eat regularly, you can fast from other things—watching the news, no-sugar-added treats, etc. There are always things from which you can fast if you are creative. Fasting increases our spiritual acuity and provides the Spirit's power deep within us.

Not only do we believers have God on the inside, but we have each other to comfort and support.

Jesus says,

> A new command I give you: Love one another. As I have loved you, so you must love one another. By this everyone will know that you are my disciples, if you love one another. (John 13:34–35)

Notice He repeats His command three times within the two verses. I'm always amazed that when I want God to change someone in my life whom I feel is difficult to love, He so often ends up renovating *my* attitude and *my* feelings toward that person. He is the one who gives us the strength and courage when we ask for it—and even sometimes when we don't ask!

In the scriptures, Paul writes a familiar passage: "And we know that in all things God works for the good of those who love him, who have been called according to his purpose" (Romans 8:28). If we really sit with this verse and allow it to seep into our pores, there is no need to remain in any form of regret, especially if we also believe that God's control of our lives is sovereign. We may make mistakes and initially feel some regret, but we don't need to stay there because we serve such an amazing God, who can turn our most profound mistakes and failures into our greatest victories. As a reminder, He took my jump and used me and the wheelchair to help over seventy people come to faith in Jesus.

You may be wondering where the good is in your situation. Truth is, you may not taste of the good in terms of feelings while you are on this earth in the physical realm. In this life, there is trouble, sometimes plenty of it, but remember that Jesus has promised Himself as *the* solution! With Him, it's all good, whether you can feel it or not. You are more than your feelings.

I'll say it again: trust God, not feelings. Proverbs 3:5–6, another set of familiar verses, says this, "Trust in the Lord with all your heart and lean not on your own understanding; in all your ways submit to him, and he will make your paths straight." These verses echo Isaiah 55:8–9, that His ways are not our ways. "For we walk by faith, not by sight" (2 Corinthians 5:7). Set your heart toward trusting Him, not indulging in and living by your feelings.

CHAPTER TWENTY-ONE
SUICIDE PREVENTION

*H*ave you ever been so heavy-hearted that you wished your life would end? If the truth were known, would you honestly answer yes to that question? Are you now tempted to bring your life to a premature close? A year or two after I had the spinal cord injury and was still deeply suicidal, a "friend" said to me, "Why don't you just commit suicide? You've been thinking about it for so long. Why don't you just go ahead and do it?"

At that moment, though I was suicidal, I found myself speechless, hesitating. In hindsight, I could see that my subconscious, at that time, was drawn toward thinking up reasons why I shouldn't end my life. It got me in touch with the part of myself that I did not think existed at the time—the part that still wanted to live. I realized that I was not—nor do I believe that anyone is ever—100 percent suicidal.

While it shocked me to hear encouragement for my suicidal thoughts, this ignited something within me—a will to live, however tiny. We need to speak gently and tenderly to those who believe they no longer want to live in order to help raise that part in them that reaches beyond their suicidality.

Perhaps you've felt as though life is not worth living, but maybe you too can sense something stirring deeply within you if you imagine someone saying the same words to you that this "friend" spoke to me.

ON INCHING FORWARD

When suicidal thoughts torment us, inching forward may be the best we can do, especially in the face of bombarding questions, like *How could I have done things differently?* or *Why did that occur?* Sometimes we can aggravate the situation by feeding into and dwelling on the negativity and denigration that ultimately come from the enemy over something that happened. Sometimes, we repeatedly mull over something that happened, desperately wishing we could retrace our steps and redo it. Some may even have a "ridiculing machine" in their minds, where self-flagellation is almost second nature. Because I was a victim of scapegoating in my childhood, that's how I felt for many years. I can still catch myself being tempted to do this. Years ago, it almost felt like a comfort to self-flagellate on an emotional level. That's what I was used to; it's where I felt "at home." If you can relate to this, does this really fit who you are as a blood-bought, infinitely precious child of the living God? If this ridiculing machine is something familiar to you, be gentle with yourself, and don't blame yourself—that's exactly what pleases the enemy. Even if whatever happened was your fault, do not feed into the negativity. Learn to let it come and go. God grieves when we give energy and fuel to the denigration. Try to keep on the sunny side, even if it's going inch by inch.

Sometimes the devil can use complex and powerful emotions to knock us off our feet. If children grow up feeling they are bad, and those are the messages they receive from their caregivers, those children may end up being nuisances on purpose because this was the way they got attention, albeit negative attention. Sometimes such children believe that negative attention is better than none. These children may tend to want to be a problem, to side with the negative messages they got and to feel okay and supported, in a twisted sense. Such children may feel no hope that they could ever be considered good, so they resign themselves to their badness. Such children may grow into adults who feed the negativity by condemning, chastising, or belittling themselves and/or others. They may find themselves believing the lies that the enemy planted so many years ago. Again though, with the help of a godly, trained professional, they can regain their footing and learn to receive more positive and accurate input into who they are as children of God. Through that process, though, they may find themselves moving forward only at an infinitesimal rate. But believe me—in the end, it all adds up, and changes can be detected over time.

I am resigned to taking one day at a time—inch by God-given inch on some days. When it comes right down to it, all we ever have is this moment. When you think about it and truly break it down to a minute-by-minute journey, handling one moment at a time is within reach. When things are crazy and/or profoundly painful, we need to set our sights on living moment by moment. As Dr. Charles Stanley says, life isn't about ease, comfort, and pleasure. It's about crawling forward, sometimes painfully scraping our elbows and knees. It's about inching forward and seeking God to direct us onward, just to the next step.

ON SURRENDER

An important step in the healing process is surrender. I reiterate Dr. M. Scott Peck's exclamation that life is difficult. Sometimes going on seems like relentless agony, virtually an impossibility. Sometimes we feel that things are not going to get better. Those who suffer with such ailments as multiple sclerosis or ALS (amyotrophic lateral sclerosis, also called Lou Gehrig's disease) as examples, bear an especially heavy load, as these conditions are generally deteriorative in nature. (As well, when you think about it, the aging process itself is deteriorative. Merely living and growing older causes health problems, sometimes very serious ones.)

Jesus was all about healing. We need to wait in hopeful anticipation of His decision to exercise His miracle-working power. Though you may not have the above-mentioned conditions, we are all on a trajectory to the inevitable and in need of healing of one sort or another. Surrender the reality of your pain, whatever form that may take, to Jesus, and don't let go of the reality of miracles. Jesus did perform them, and He can still choose to do so today. He is able to totally eradicate all pain in your life. Never lose sight of this hope. Keeping the possibility of miracles in our minds—whether we've been given a terminal diagnosis, suffer from a painful chronic condition, or have profound family issues—can give us hope and support, even if worse comes to worst, and the miracle of healing never comes to pass. If you should choose to end your life prematurely, you rob God of the potential opportunity to heal you.

Bear in mind that scripture does say that Jesus healed "many" (Mark 1:34; 3:10), not all. It is possible that God may choose to keep you in your present condition. He may improve and heal, or He may allow the status quo, even deterioration. Ultimately, we are all in His sovereign hands. Can we rest in that fact?

Hanging on to the thought that Jesus may choose to heal is not wrong, as long as it doesn't impede your ability to accept and surrender the reality of your pain to His sovereign will, whatever He may choose to do. Remember that scripture does not say "in some things" but "in *all* things, God works for the good of those who love him, who have been called according to his purpose" (Romans 8:28; italics mine). Whatever He decides to do in your situation, know the result will be for your ultimate good, even if it doesn't feel that way at the time. Simply know that He will use it for His glory, no matter what the situation, as you give it all to Him. Love Him by surrendering all to Jesus. To love Him is to let Him help you.

Maybe something horrible has happened to you, and you find yourself blaming God for what happened. That was me when I was newly injured, especially when I went to live in the institution. Despite my expressing rage and bitterness toward Him, and in fact cursing Him, as I've said, He graciously continued to work in me. He eventually restored my faith and built it up stronger than had I not jumped. If you are in a place of blaming God, know that He understands. Trust though, that He is working in you as a born-again believer regardless.

God helped me to see, as I surrendered my pain to Him, that it better equipped me to serve others. My suffering makes me better equipped for God to use me as an instrument of truth and a more credible comforter to those in deep and relentless agony (2 Corinthians 1:3–4). Second Corinthians 1:5 says, "For just as we share abundantly in the sufferings of Christ, so also our comfort abounds through Christ." Notice Paul again speaks about deep trouble as something we are to see as normal in this life.

As I laid down my burden, God's comfort trickled, then poured in and through me to others. My struggle involves laying down self-will and self-direction. This surrender allows me to access more fully His omnipotent nature, "for the battle is the Lord's" (1 Samuel 17:47) and "for the battle is not yours, but God's" (2 Chronicles 20:15b). Letting Him carry me is a privilege of being a child of God. I'm reminded here again of the prose, "Footprints."

Let Him and His strength carry *you* as you lay down your burdens at the foot of the cross. Someone wise once told me to do just that—and to not pick them up again. How often do we lay them down, only to retrieve them in frustration at God's timing or His seeming "incompetence" or inability to solve our problems in the way we think He should? Remember, God's ways are not our own (Isaiah 55:8–9). They are unique to Him, the eternal Creator. Who better to surrender our trials and our pains to than our Creator Himself? Let God be God in your life. Let Him be the mystery that He is. Just trust in faith—something that is sometimes very difficult to do.

Friend, your body may remain in its broken state or maybe that choice that brought so much pain cannot be undone, but God will heal the inner brokenness, your spirit, as you surrender your suffering to Him—all of it. It may take years to adjust to your injury (as it did for me) or to the condition in which you find yourself. In the following section, I would like to introduce you to an inspiring friend of mine, and then we will look into the scripture to further illustrate this point.

Chapter Twenty-two
MORE ON SURRENDER

KAREN BOOTH

I had a friend named Karen Booth, who has since passed on into glory. She had lived in the same institution I was in, residing there for twenty-two years. She had had a stroke three days after she had open-heart surgery at the age of thirty-eight; as a result, she became unable to use her hands, her vocal cords, or her legs, and she was virtually blind. Her mind, though, remained sharp and bright.

In order to communicate, she had a laminated paper attached to her wheelchair that had the alphabet separated into three sections. I would ask her from which section the first letter of the first word she wanted to communicate came. She would indicate section one, two, or three with a nod or a shake of her head. She did this with each letter of each word she wanted to say.

She could mouth certain letters, so those very close to her could communicate with her faster. As a strong believer in God, she had come to fully accept her lot in life and had completely surrendered it to Jesus. She forged ahead, one day at a time. She was robbed of privacy and foundational quiet on a daily basis; although Karen had a single room, doors at the institution remained open virtually at all times for staff monitoring of patients. In addition, she regularly had to endure mistreatment from the nurses on staff there. She also had severe family issues. Despite all this, she most often greeted me with a smile and laughter when I would visit. She had a great big, grateful heart!

Karen died from an infection in her blood just as I was making the final edit on the original compilation of this book, published in 2008. She remains a testament to the resilience of the human spirit and to the power of God's Spirit living within an individual. She remains an inspiration to me, as God used her brokenness and her courage to inspire me and others. Don't doubt that He can do the same with yours.

PAUL

Remember, three times Paul actually "pleaded" (2 Corinthians 12:8) for the "thorn in … [his] flesh" (2 Corinthians 12:7) to be taken from him, though Paul did not specify what that "thorn" was. Choosing not to remove it, Jesus simply replied, "My grace is sufficient for you, for my power is made perfect in weakness" (2 Corinthians 12:9a). I imagine that Paul felt quite frustrated, perhaps even angry, about this, particularly when God first spoke this to him. Perhaps it took Paul some time and work to accept God's will for him, regarding his thorn.

Take all the time you need, and grieve the losses that come with your thorn. God may not take your suffering away, but He will give you the grace to endure it, if you will trust Him with it (although that's easier said than done).

Paul emphatically goes on:

> Therefore I will boast all the more gladly about my weaknesses, so that Christ's power may rest on me.

> That is why, for Christ's sake, I delight in weaknesses, in insults, in hardships, in persecution, in difficulties.

> For when I am weak, then I am strong. (2 Corinthians 12:9b–10)

We need not fear trouble or approach it with disdain. We can follow in Paul's footsteps and even be glad when weakness of any kind hits us, as God will use it to make us more into His likeness (2 Corinthians 3:18). Regarding his challenges, Paul actually boasts about his sufferings, including the seemingly outrageous, "If I must boast, I will boast of the things that show my weakness" (2 Corinthians 11:30). This goes against everything the world values in a man—power, strength, virility. In embracing his weakness, Paul was given these qualities and could exclaim that he was "strong" in his weakness. As a reminder, Paul was in prison when he wrote that he had learned to be content "in any and every situation" (Philippians 4:12). Scripture doesn't speak directly of Paul's surrendering his suffering to Christ, but from this verse, it is highly likely. By following Paul's example, we too can find great strength. Not only Paul, but Jesus led us in His ability to surrender all.

It strikes me that Jesus surrendered His place on the throne next to the Father to come down to earth as a weak, helpless baby to sin-prone parents. He surrendered His will in the garden of Gethsemane, basically saying these words twice: "My Father, if it is possible, may this cup be taken from me. Yet not as I will, but as you will" (Matthew 26:39b, 42). Surrendering His reputation, He endured mockery and physical brutality.

> Those who passed by hurled insults at him, shaking their heads and saying, "You who are going to destroy the temple and build it in three days, save yourself! Come down from the cross, if you are the Son of God!" (Matthew 27:39–40)

> The men who were guarding Jesus began mocking and beating him. They blindfolded him and demanded, "Prophesy! Who hit you?" And they said many other insulting things to him. (Luke 22:63–65)

In addition, Jesus finally relinquished His body to unimaginable viciousness, more beatings, floggings, and, eventually, a slow, excruciating death on a cruel Roman cross. It was the will of the Father that He might provide the way for us to be saved from eternal horror. Jesus embraced and surrendered His suffering, and in the process, He released spiritual power for us to receive, simply for the asking. As the song says, "There is power, power, wonder-working power in the precious blood of the Lamb." Like with Jesus, we need to surrender our lives and our will to His in order for Him to release that power.

CHAPTER TWENTY-THREE
I AM RICHER

J am richer now and for all eternity because of my suffering. I will
share with you a passage that has become so dear to my heart.

> But whatever were gains to me I now consider loss for the sake
> of Christ. What is more, I consider everything a loss because of
> the surpassing worth of knowing Christ Jesus my Lord, for whose
> sake I have lost all things.
>
> I consider them garbage, that I may gain Christ and be found in
> him, not having a righteousness of my own that comes from the
> law, but that which is through faith in Christ—the righteousness
> that comes from God on the basis of faith.
>
> I want to know Christ—yes, to know the power of his resurrection
> and participation in his sufferings, becoming like him in his
> death, and so, somehow, attaining to the resurrection from the
> dead. (Philippians 3:7–11)

I in no way wish to appear as though I am putting myself on a level with
the great apostle Paul, but I agree with him that everything that does not help
me know Christ is like refuse to me. That I may gain Him in my character

is of such eternal value that I cannot fully grasp here on this earth, yet one day I will know. Experiencing and sharing in His sufferings gets me closer to Him, as I reach to let God use them to draw me nearer. It helps me to relate to Him better now and when I get to heaven. I am richer in my understanding of God's pain and am richer in my ability to relate to Him and empathize with His creation—people, people in pain.

Give Him time to work in you and in the situation. You too will find yourself richer for it, both now and then. Realize that you will be spending a lot more time with Him on the other side of eternity than you will here. As a reminder, as author and pastor Rick Warren says, this life is but a preparation for the next. I have a friend who says, "One day, we will laugh!" God is much bigger than you are. He's much bigger than your problems, and can thoroughly handle all of them—believe that!

THOUGHTS ON SUICIDE

If you wish to prepare for some unknown time in the future when you think you might experience thoughts of suicide, as a reminder:

> Therefore, since we have a great high priest who has ascended into heaven, Jesus the Son of God, let us hold firmly to the faith we profess.
>
> For we do not have a high priest who is unable to empathize with our weaknesses, but we have one who has been tempted in every way, just as we are—yet he did not sin.
>
> Let us then approach God's throne of grace with confidence, so that we may receive mercy and find grace to help us in our time of need. (Hebrews 4:14–16)

Jesus knows your pain. Although it doesn't directly say it in the scripture, perhaps the devil was tempting Jesus at Gethsemane with thoughts of suicide. What if Jesus had given in to them? He knows the pain of someone with suicidal thoughts. Know that you can, therefore, trust Him with them. He promises help and rest, as only He can do (Matthew 11:28–30), here on earth, but He assures us of true love and eternal freedom in the afterlife as well. I had a Christian friend who believed that if she committed suicide, she would go to hell. Scripture, however, clearly says that no one can snatch you from His hand (John 10:28b) and that Christians cannot be separated from the love of God (Romans 8:38–39). There is not one verse or commandment that says, "You shall not kill yourself." There is, however, the sixth commandment: "You shall not murder" (Deuteronomy 5:17; Exodus 20:13). It has been said that suicide is murder of self and, therefore, a sin.

Though I consider suicide to be a sin, it is forgivable. Be gentle with yourself if you have made an attempt in the past. For the future, realize that once saved always saved. While I believe with Dr. Charles Stanley in eternal security, it is nothing to take advantage of or bank on because we want an exit from our pain. We can glean strength from the endurance of Jesus by making the following our prayer: "May the Lord direct … [our] hearts into God's love and Christ's perseverance" (2 Thessalonians 3:5).

When we hurt ourselves, in whatever way, whether it's to demean ourselves, cut ourselves, or the ultimate, suicide, we hurt His creation (John 1:3)—His creation, whom He called "very good" (Genesis 1:31a), His creation, who is "fearfully and wonderfully made" (Psalm 139:14a).

Destroying yourself is not honoring God (1 Corinthians 6:19–20). Remember, you are His possession. Just as we did not create ourselves and will ourselves into being, the way we leave this world needs to be left up to Him and His will. *Your* life is really not your own to take. I would say that the most intimate and personal parts of you are intricately connected to your loved ones and friends, but more on that later.

Children of abusers can get stuck in their pain and wish to retaliate against their parents, if their parents were the perpetrators. Consider your motives for suicide.

> Do not take revenge, my dear friends, but leave room for God's wrath, for it is written: "It is mine to avenge; I will repay," says the Lord.
> On the contrary:
> "If your enemy is hungry, feed him;
> if he is thirsty, give him something to drink.
> In doing this, you will heap burning coals on his head."
> Do not be overcome by evil, but overcome evil with good. (Romans 12:19–21)

Another example of the radical love of God! Certainly, Jesus Himself said, "You have heard that it was said, 'Love your neighbor and hate your enemy.' But I tell you, love your enemies and pray for those who persecute you, that you may be children of your Father in heaven" (Matthew 5:43–45). Being His children, we are expected to behave as such, no matter how hard it is to do, no matter what's been done to us.

If you have felt or fear that you, in the future, might feel helpless to the point of wanting to end your life, know that you are not alone. Many have felt this way. I have felt this way so very many times. In the early years of my being diagnosed with a biochemical imbalance in my brain, I spent much time feeling suicidal, years again. It was only as I grew and matured as a Christian and as a sufferer of depression over time that I was able to leave those thoughts behind— barring acute mental sickness, mind you. This is why it is so important that you exercise patience with God if you are or are prone to becoming suicidal.

In the life of every adult, there may come a time when he or she thinks of suicide. Know that no one has an ideal life. Everyone suffers. Even the rich and famous, whom we can envy, have problems: paparazzi hound them, and they live under the microscope of public scrutiny.

Dr. Charles Stanley says that nothing happens that is outside of God's permissive will. Know that you are in His hand and that He is in control. Feelings of hopelessness, whenever they may arise, are not a surprise to Him, but they are just that—feelings that change with the tide of emotion that rises and recedes within us. Feelings like that belong at the foot of the cross. Give them to Him. Let Him take them and—I say again--carry you. He can then perform miracles in your heart that only He can do. Thoughts of suicide and the act itself are truly the enemy's work (John 10:10).

As we prepare for whatever life brings, in our moments of deep despair, we need to reach out to Jesus, who cares for us in an eternal kind of way—a way so big and so high that you and I cannot possibly fully grasp.

CHAPTER TWENTY-FOUR

IN THE CASE OF MENTAL ILLNESS

As a reminder, many mental illnesses are merely biochemical disorders of the brain that require medicine. Mental illness of any sort—major depression, bipolar disorder (manic depression), schizophrenia, or obsessive-compulsive disorder, to name a few—can wreak severe havoc in the life of the sufferer. Suicidal ideation can be a symptom with these types of disorders. For sufferers to be and stay informed about their particular mental illness, they need to engage with a competent professional, as was modeled in the movie *A Beautiful Mind*. John Nash had the support and understanding of his psychiatrist. This is so crucial, as the mentally ill person can be like a vulnerable child—Little Red Riding Hood lost in the woods, with a wolf chasing her. The ill person, though, needs to be able to articulate if and when he or she experiences suicidal thoughts. Certainly, part of the responsibility still rests on the sick one.

Often, what is needed is to have a corporate hand of love extended. Understandably, friends and relatives may not know what to say or do (topics addressed in the coming sections), but the one who is ill needs those around him or her to be actively loving, not merely passively watching and waiting, hoping the person deals with the illness on his or her own or that it just goes away. The very nature of mental illness is that it can incapacitate sufferers to the point where they cannot recognize that they are ill. Family and friends need to step in and insist that the person gets the care he or she needs, going with the person to the emergency department of their local hospital, if necessary.

There may be a tendency for professionals to hurry the patient through the emergency room visit, placate the patient, and send him or her "off to bed with milk and cookies." If the patient verbalizes a specific plan of suicide, he or she should be taken very seriously and be admitted to the hospital. Sadly, verbalizing a plan of suicide is no guarantee of admission to the hospital.

In my case, a week prior to my jump, I explicitly expressed to one emergency room doctor that unless I was hospitalized, I intended to leap from a specific bridge, known for its lethality. In fact, during that week, three hospitals were aware of my fear that I would try to end my life in this fashion. Instead of hospitalization, the professionals sent me twice to a psychiatric holding center that was walking distance from the very bridge I had named. This center was not equipped to deal with someone who was actively suicidal.

Beds in the psych ward are often at a premium, but practitioners should take their roles seriously. A person in acute psychiatric sickness requires the professional's strong and supportive hand to lead him or her through the maze of mental illness and back to health.

WHAT TO SAY

Family members who notice unusual behavior in their ill relative ought to be on the alert and make concerted attempts to protect their relative. People often admit, "I didn't know what to say," when confronted with a person with a serious condition, such as acute mental illness. This is understandable; being in the presence of someone in a great deal of pain can cause even the most eloquent to stumble over their words.

I would suggest speaking from your heart. Tell the ill one that you feel tongue-tied. Reiterate your love, if that's appropriate, and concern. Say it directly, with carefully chosen words. Don't assume that the ill person should know your feelings toward him or her. Those who are ill need to hear from you; love can be so motivating and healing. You can say how you feel when seeing the ill one in his or her condition. Say you feel desperate, sad, helpless, confused—speak your heart.

Try not to dismiss the ill person or write him or her off—that's the worst thing you could do. Enter in, take heart, and be a friend to the wounded one—he or she is not so different from you. The root cause of his or her problem may be as simple as a biochemical imbalance that requires a specific type of medication, as was the case with me at the time of the jump. A few months after it, I fired my psychiatrist at the time with the help of my dear mom and requested a new one. The now late Dr. Edward Kingstone was assigned to me. He finally prescribed the antipsychotic pills I needed when I told him, "I'm going to do it again if the voices don't stop." When I felt better after being on the antipsychotics for a short period, I wanted to go off of them. He said, "I'm going on vacation. We'll assess the situation when I return in two weeks." When he returned, I wanted more of the drug! The medication made the difference between night and day. The meds eliminated the tormenting voices and brought me back into reality.

With the mentally ill, even professionals sometimes have difficulty asking the proper questions. If there is some confusion about a client's state of mind, a psychiatrist might say to the ill one something like, "Describe the world you live in." Once a diagnosis has been determined, it is important that the patient realizes that his or her perhaps skewed thinking is a symptom of mental illness.

There is a stream of counseling that suggests that the professional go along with an ill person's strange ideas; this, however, is tantamount to enabling and encouraging the illness. In the movie *A Beautiful Mind*, John Nash was delusional. It was through the help of his psychiatrist that he recovered. Clinicians need to pay attention to what they hear, and if what they hear is beyond their expertise to diagnose—that is, if they are social workers, chaplains, or caseworkers—they should get a psychiatrist involved, for the sake—for perhaps for the very lives—of their clients. I was working with a chaplain on a weekly basis for nine months of my delusional period, prior to the jump. As you may have guessed, she chose to go along with my strange ideas and did not seek the counsel of someone more trained to help. Maybe it's becoming clearer to you how important a competent psychiatrist is in the life of a sufferer of mental illness.

Remember that most often, suicidal ideation is a symptom of a mental illness. The suicidal person is asking, "Do I matter?" The best way to answer yes is to say it with action as well as with words. You may think you have shown that they matter, but in times of acute mental illness, those who are ill should be certain of it. Again, reaffirm your care and concern for the sufferer. The "voices" that may be regularly bombarding the ill person's mind may denigrate and put down the sufferer to the point where his or her self-esteem is significantly marred, if not eliminated. Realize that a barrage of strange thoughts can also paralyze the ill one. Prepare yourself by learning to articulate your feelings so that if this test comes along, you will better know how to help prevent possible tragedy. Knowing what to do is just as important as knowing what to say.

WHAT TO DO

If your relative or friend is behaving in an odd, out-of-character way, explain directly to that person that you are concerned about the behavior, and suggest that you and that person speak about it with a doctor. Educate yourself regarding the symptoms of the person's specific condition, and go with him or her to the clinician and/or the hospital, and discuss the behavior you've seen. If the doctor is a general practitioner, request a referral to a psychiatrist, and, again, go with the sufferer to that appointment. I realize this may be a lot to ask, but the very life of the sufferer may hang in the balance.

If the ill one expresses suicidal ideation, a question you could ask him or her is, "How would you do it?" If the person in distress directly verbalizes a plan of suicide, once again, he or she needs a protected, safe environment, with access to specially trained psychiatric professionals, both doctors and nurses, who can offer specific emotional and psychiatric support (e.g., hospitalization on a psychiatric ward). These folks are especially trained in dealing with every type of disorder, from mood disorders, to personality, anxiety and eating disorders, to full-blown psychoses of every form. Do not settle for anything less than admission for your suicidal friend or relative, especially if he or she has a plan in mind.

CHAPTER TWENTY-FIVE

IN THE CASE OF PSYCHOSIS, AN ADVOCATE IS NECESSARY

As a reminder, psychosis blinds the mind of the sufferer as to the reality of his or her condition—indeed, to external reality in general—to the point where the ill one will not realize that he or she is not well. For this reason, the ill one needs an advocate to ensure he or she can get the treatment he or she needs and deserves. The advocate can be a professional, such as a social worker or case manager, or a loved one or friend. Remember that it is so important not to dismiss those who are ill, as if they are responsible for and in control of their conditions. Can a cancer patient make himself better? Should a person with "cancer of the mind" be expected to take full responsibility for himself?

It is important, however, that the ill one embrace and try to be as proactive as possible with regard to his or her mental illness. Often, those with psychiatric conditions can take control and seek suitable treatment for themselves when they are well. They need to understand their symptoms, and when they notice them crop up, they can go for help before the symptoms escalate. If symptoms are left unaddressed, full-blown psychosis can take hold, and the person cannot be held responsible.

A fall into mental illness, including psychosis, is unlikely if the sufferer faithfully takes his or her prescribed medication, but medication can lose its effectiveness over time, and may need to be adjusted.

If you are a loved one or friend who has been approached to become an advocate, be sure to educate yourself on the signs and symptoms of psychosis with regard to the specific illness of the sufferer, so that you can step in, should things get to that stage. I can't stress enough that you, as the advocate, should *not* settle for anything less than what you feel the ill one needs. Do not be shy about impressing your concerns to professionals. Perseverance and assertiveness from the advocate, as well as from the sufferer if possible, can break through the barriers to treatment.

I pray that you can help your friend or loved one, so that he or she might be protected and kept safe in times of acute mental illness. Suicidal ideation can be present with psychosis; this is all the more reason why the ill one needs an advocate.

Remember that death is eternal. Death is a one-shot deal. People with mental illness can be fighting for their lives. Unless they have a battle plan, a firm understanding of the spiritual nature of the war they are in (Ephesians 6:12), and an advocate, in my opinion, the illness can lead them to act out on thoughts of self-harm, as the pain can be just that intense.

I feel we would tend to be more understanding with regard to suicide if that act came from someone who is, for example, in a wheelchair. We could see, physically, the reason for the person's despair. But do we accept it as readily from someone who is mentally ill? We cannot visually see the root of the torment. Yet the torment of suicidal ideation can be with or without the presence of psychosis, and it remains a real killer.

THE NATURE OF "SUICIDALITY" IN MENTAL ILLNESS

"Suicidality" in mental illness can be felt as strongly as a need. The devil can cause it to be so very strong that it can consume a person. Suicidal thoughts can become a panacea for the enormous pain of the illness. Contemplating suicide seriously can provide relief from a world that is fraught with the seemingly unending torment of mental illness. Satan tries to wear a person out with a constant barrage of emotional and spiritual pain. Especially in the case of psychosis, it can be very exhausting, for it tends to take the sufferer into another world, which is sometimes exciting but often terrifying, again, as a reminder.

Suicidality in mental illness is most often the result of misinformation and the confused thinking that goes along with the illness. This is why it is so crucial for those who suffer with mental illness to educate themselves regarding their specific conditions. This is also why pharmaceuticals are so important; the one with the illness needs to be aware that meds may be the answer for what ails him or her. If your mentally ill friend or relative is under the care of a psychiatrist, and you still see symptoms, especially suicidal ideation, after some time, I encourage you to get a second opinion.

Again, if illness in your loved one is acute, don't be shy about taking a proactive stance. We want to catch those who are ill before tragedy strikes, and they make a decision to act on a plan of suicide. Keen observation, especially by clinicians, protection, and advocacy are all essential with regard to dealing with one who is suicidal.

AFTER A SUICIDE ATTEMPT

We need to be careful to respond to those around us in love. Remember that Jesus says three separate times, in the span of only two verses, that we are to "love one another" (John 13:34–35). In fact, He calls it a command! If a loved one or friend has survived a suicide attempt, tell that person how you feel about it, and affirm that person's worth and value in your life. It is not loving to avoid or ignore the person or the issue; don't use the excuse that you don't know what to say. Sadly, so many people chose that route after my attempts.

Say something like, "I feel so sad that I couldn't help you before. I experienced guilt and loneliness and helplessness when you tried to take your life. I can imagine these difficult feelings would have been so amplified if you had succeeded. I cannot imagine my life with you forever gone from it. You are needed, are valuable to me and are infinitely precious to God. Your life means more than I can put into words. Please try to go on. I'll do what I can to help you."

We may need to be reminded what love is: "Love is patient, love is kind … it keeps no record of wrongs" (1 Corinthians 13:4a, 5b). If you love the one who made the attempt, make a special effort to show it. Do not hold the desperate act against the person or blame him or her for the hurt he or she caused you. Someone who tries to commit suicide is not thinking clearly to begin with; he or she doesn't consider the psychological ramifications of the attempt on those around him or her.

Work through your grief and/or guilt, forgive the person, and then, reach out to him or her with that forgiveness. Let the pain that surrounds your loved one's attempt spur you to action to help that person find inner resources so that there won't be another attempt in the future. Those who try to kill themselves are in deep pain and are crying out. Respond with this powerfully healing thing called love, by way of honesty and courage. Then, they may find the strength to pick themselves up, forgive themselves (such a tough step), and begin again to carry on.

CHAPTER TWENTY-SIX

ON JESUS AND JOY

Rejoice in the Lord always.
—Philippians 4:4

Note here that Paul does not say simply here, "Rejoice always," or "Rejoice in our circumstances"; he says, "Rejoice in the *Lord* always" (italics mine). Particularly in tough times, we need to remind ourselves of the eternal joy and bliss He bought for us on Calvary—experiences we will share fully with Him when our time comes to meet him face-to-face. Not only do we have this incredible hope, but we have Him with us every moment of every day and on into eternity! He will never leave us. He has given the Holy Spirit to indwell, guide, and comfort us always. We certainly do have much to rejoice about!

More from Paul:

Therefore, having been justified by faith, we have peace with God through our Lord Jesus Christ, through whom also we have access by faith into this grace in which we stand, and rejoice in hope of the glory of God.

And not only that, but we also glory in tribulations, knowing that tribulation produces perseverance; and perseverance, character; and character, hope.

Now hope does not disappoint, because the love of God has been poured out in our hearts by the Holy Spirit who was given to us. (Romans 5:1–5 NKJV)

It is so amazing that suffering, or *tribulation*, is juxtaposed with the word *hope* and with the idea that "the love of God has been poured out in our hearts." Could it be that God is going to accomplish this in and through your suffering in a way that He could not do any other way? And could it be that what God has allowed in our lives is purely because He loves us so much? Could it be? Recall, however, that much of what we are asked to suffer is a process. Jesus Himself, at Gethsemane, did not immediately arrive at willingness to take on the sin of the world and the cross. He pleaded with His Father and with His disciples each several times when his soul was "exceedingly sorrowful" (Matthew 26:38 NKJV). Can we face our Gethsemanes, with the help of the strength and power of Jesus, and embrace that which God is asking us to endure? Or should we run? Just look at what the Father accomplished through the faithfulness and perseverance of Jesus.

In line with Paul and to remind you, James says this:

Consider it pure joy, my brothers and sisters, whenever you face trials of many kinds, because you know that the testing of your faith produces perseverance.

Let perseverance finish its work so that you may be mature and complete, not lacking anything. (James 1:2–4)

And to reiterate, here's Peter:

Dear friends, do not be surprised at the fiery ordeal that has come on you to test you, as though something strange were happening to you.

> But rejoice inasmuch as you participate in the sufferings of Christ, so that you may be overjoyed when his glory is revealed. (1 Peter 4:12–13)

Take heart, friend. As you look to Jesus with trust, He can change your inner cursing to shouts of joy with His blessings of strength and love poured into your heart, as the scripture says. Notice that I did not say *happiness* but *joy*, as happiness is based on circumstances. Happiness comes and goes, but the joy of Jesus persists, even through the most difficult and painful of circumstances.

Joy is a fruit of the Spirit (see Galatians 5:22–23) that God can mold into any heart that is open and willing to endure the pruning. Jesus Himself said,

> I am the true vine, and my Father is the gardener.
>
> He cuts off every branch in me that bears no fruit, while every branch that does bear fruit, he prunes so that it will be even more fruitful. (John 15:1–2)

Endure the pruning. Rail and fuss if you must, but endure the pruning in the end. On your judgment day, when all will be finally made clear, including God's full reasons and purposes for your individual suffering, you will be eternally glad you did.

CHAPTER TWENTY-SEVEN
THE POWER OF PRAYER

*D*espair is the very soil from which rich prayer *can* grow. Admittedly, however, it can be very difficult to pray while in despair because of sheer exhaustion. You may be tempted to collapse in a heap with no more than a whimper and a sob, if this describes you. Gather your strength and do your utmost to cry out to God. He is especially attentive to you at this time: "The Lord is close to the brokenhearted and saves those who are crushed in spirit" (Psalm 34:18). Say that you feel so spent that you are barely able to articulate what you feel. Ask Him for His courage. With God's help, He can give you the spiritual power to build those prayer muscles so that, even in the darkest times, you can find it in yourself to reach to Him.

In those times, however, when the words just don't come, and you truly cannot muster prayer yourself, let God use the despair to urge you to reach out and enlist the prayers of others on your behalf. When you feel down, you need to be covered in a spiritual blanket of prayer from the body of Christ.

When you are in despair, you are vulnerable to dwelling in negativity; if you know, however, that you are being lifted up to God by other Christians, this may be the jump-start you need to press on into healing and to begin again to pray for yourself. If you find yourself in despair, God, if you will allow Him, will use this painful emotion for His purposes. Let Him use it to teach you.

Remember, "Seek and you *will* find" (italics mine), perhaps not in the material but in the spiritual realm.

> Those who know your name trust in you, for you, LORD, have
> never forsaken those who seek you. (Psalm 9:10)

Whether you find yourself in the throes of despair or not, prayer is the hinge on which decisions should swing.

Jesus knew the power of prayer to heal and to comfort, as well as the power in the petition itself. This can be extended as a warning to those with suicidal thoughts or tendencies. Know that it is Satan who tempts us to give up.

> When tempted, no one should say, "God is tempting me."

> For God cannot be tempted by evil, nor does he tempt anyone.
> (James 1:13)

In the garden of Gethsemane, Jesus was able to pray, though in great grief and pain. He cried out, "My soul is overwhelmed with sorrow to the point of death" (Matthew 26:38a). In the movie *The Passion of the Christ,* at this point in Jesus's journey to the cross, Satan is depicted as speaking with Jesus, telling him that the weight of the sin of the world is too great for Him. Though the scripture does not directly speak to this, likely the devil *was* taunting the Lord when Jesus was in great need Himself. Certainly, in the temptations of Christ, "after fasting forty days and forty nights, [when] he was hungry" (Matthew 4:2), Satan came to him and told him to produce bread if He was, in fact, the Son of God. That's the way the devil works; he seeks to weaken us with relentless struggle, and when we are in deep need, he comes at us and plants sometimes horrific thoughts in our minds. The key is to stay close to Jesus in times of ongoing, agonizing difficulty so we can avoid being worn out to the point where we start listening to the thoughts Satan produces.

The Lord is not unacquainted with deep struggle; in fact, as He accepted the cup that held the full weight of sin, He had known more struggle than we will ever face. He knows what you are going through in *your* garden of Gethsemane. Won't you reach to Him? Won't you cry out to Him?

Lift up your issues to He who knows and loves you, or, as Peter so aptly put it, "Cast all your anxiety on him because he cares for you" (1 Peter 5:7). Get others involved on your behalf, and watch God work as you feel your helplessness drain from you. You can pray about all the issues over which you have no control. That's one way to take power back. Give up the control of the situation to God. He knows all and has the power to remedy it, should He choose to do so. Just know that His activity or seeming inactivity following prayer is completely up to Him and His sovereign will. Remember, as well, that He is, at His core, a mystery to our finite minds. Regardless of whether He chooses to act or not to act in your situation, there is profound healing power in the very practice of prayer.

WE ALL NEED HELP

We all need help, at certain times more than at others. In the garden of Gethsemane, even Jesus reached both vertically to the Father and horizontally to the disciples. The Bible says that He went with His disciples to the garden and specifically asked Peter and the two sons of Zebedee, "Stay here and keep watch with me" (Matthew 26:38b). Then, looking up, "he fell with his face to the ground and prayed, 'My Father, if it is possible, may this cup be taken from me'" (Matthew 26:39b).

Then Jesus went back to His disciples and found they had not kept watch, as He had asked. After speaking to them, Jesus returned to the Father and prayed again, "Your will be done" (Matthew 26:42b). He then made His way back to the disciples again and found them asleep. One can only imagine the temptations to disappointment and discouragement He felt at this point. Twice he went to his disciples for support and they let him down.

Following this, He returned one more time to the Father. Finally, He went once again to the disciples to speak to them. Notice Jesus modeling this back-and-forth movement for us when He is, again, "overwhelmed with sorrow to the point of death" (Matthew 26:38a). Even Jesus, who was 100 percent divine as well as 100 percent human, went repeatedly not only to His Father but to his disciples in His deep hour of need. How much more do we need Him? How much more do we need each other? Even Job had friends he could talk to, who listened to him and allowed him to have his say, as they had theirs, though what they said may not have been the most helpful, to say the least.

Jesus, through His process, developed the strength to be able to say to His Father, "Yet not as I will, but as you will" (Matthew 26:39). If you have felt that life is not worth living, know that if God wanted you in heaven with Him, He could take you. You are here for a reason. Maybe you are tempted to give up. If Jesus had given up in His garden of Gethsemane, we would not have the Savior of the world. He showed us how to persevere.

God wants to use you in your pain, as He did with Jesus in His pain. Perhaps He wants to make you a savior (with a small *s*) in His plan to bring others to Him, to comfort and encourage others as they see His strength and light in you. This is what happened with my dear dad and me when he was in his seventy-ninth year.

Won't you look to God and let Him give you the strength to pray, "Yet not as I will, but as You will"? Let God be God in your life.

I don't know what was more devastating for Jesus—the separation from His Father as He atoned for all sin, or the agony and torture of the cross. All this—ponder it a moment—He did for you. You are worth that much. Won't you give back to Him your heart, your life, your death? Your natural death you can give to Jesus as a precious gift in response to all He has done for you.

You cannot control other people and their reactions to you, but you can choose to look to the only sinless one to find both the strength and provision for yourself, particularly in dark times. Trust in the words of the song by Stuart Townend and Keith Getty, "In Christ Alone." They say that in Christ alone, their hope is found, that Jesus is firm through the worst drought and storm, and that He is their all-in-all.

Don't be afraid to stand apart from others, even if they are family members and it comes down to only Jesus by your side. The movie *A Man for All Seasons* is based on the life of Sir Thomas More, who stood up for Christ to the point of death, despite the pleadings of his family to relent. (Incidentally, it won the Best Picture Oscar in 1966.)

Look to omnipotence and to supportive others interdependently, for we all need help.

CHAPTER TWENTY-EIGHT
GOING ON IS TOUGHER

I knew an older woman in the institution who was paralyzed from the waist down. She was also partially blind and partially deaf. She tried to starve herself to death. What turned her around was her grandchild, who said to her, "What kind of an example are you setting for us, Grandma?"

I said to her, "Taking your life takes great courage."

She said, "Going on is tougher."

You may be feeling as this woman did. If so, I encourage you to hang in there. Just as God did with Job, He can turn things around for you; if you fail to press on and give in to the temptation of ending your life, you forfeit the opportunity for God to do this.

THE TWO GREAT COMMANDMENTS

Yes, life is tough. That is why we have been given commandments to guide and strengthen us. Jesus said that the "most important" (Mark 12:29), "the first and greatest" (Matthew 22:38) commandment is, "Love the Lord your God with all your heart and with all your soul and with all your mind and with all your strength" (Matthew 22:37; Mark 12:30). Love involves trust, and trust involves faith. We need to reach out in love and to have trust and faith that God—in His sovereign wisdom and seeing things, as He does, from an eternal perspective— knows what He is doing by allowing our suffering.

The second greatest commandment (Matthew 22:39; Mark 12:31) is this: "Love your neighbor as yourself," which appears numerous times in the New Testament to show just how important a teaching it is (Matthew 19:19, Luke 10:27, Romans 13:9, Galatians 5:14, James 2:8, as examples). Again, you are commanded not only to love your neighbor but also yourself. Hurting yourself is not loving yourself. When it comes down to it, it may feel that suicide is an act of loving yourself because you think it will get you out of your pain, but feelings are changeable. Powerful though they may be, it is unwise to act on feelings. Instead, let God love you whole, in His way.

It can be very hard work to take good care of ourselves. Keeping up with the furious pace of life is, in itself, a talent. I find that my inner equilibrium and peace can be rocked as I go through my day. I have to reach to God again and again for strength and help, as Satan repeatedly tries to knock me off balance. The devil never gives up; he can be relentless. I understand that we can get very tired.

FATIGUE

Fatigue can be an indication that something is wrong with your body and that you are, in fact, ill. If this is the case, it's wise to seek medical attention.

However, fatigue may also be used by the enemy to deceive. How often do your eyes feel heavy when you are doing your morning devotionals? Fatigue also can be a barrier to doing good works. It can make you believe that you can't make it; that you can't play that game with the kids; that you can't do that extra report; that you can't engage in that heart-to-heart that someone asked of you; that you can't do the work of unpacking your feelings about a troubling situation; that you can't pray or read your Bible.

It seems that sometimes, the more we give in to fatigue, the more our frail human bodies crave rest. We lie down for a nap, only to find it brutal to get up, even hours later. We can go on vacation, only to come home and feel like we need to rest after our rest!

Sometimes we are challenged to go on less sleep than we think we need or less than we are used to getting. When we are put to this kind of test, it can demonstrate just how resilient a human spirit can be to adjust to the ever-changing, challenging circumstances in which we find ourselves. As we lean more heavily on Him, He proves Himself faithful.

I always have needed a lot of sleep; I usually get around ten hours per night. When I lived in the institution, I went on much less sleep than I was used to getting. Because it was required that the doors to our rooms remained open, the noise at night would inevitably produce interrupted sleep. Plus, we were wakened for procedures during the night. I could not nap during the day, as the noise from the hallways and the lights overhead were constant. Still, God gave me the strength to go on each day.

Granted, we all have good and bad days—days when we are soaring and flying high, and days when the blues come knocking, and fatigue tempts us to retreat. I believe that this is just part of the natural ebb and flow of life. Disappointments will surely come, and when they do, they can add to our sense of fatigue, but remember the words of Dr. Charles Stanley: "Disappointment is inevitable. Discouragement is a choice."

With fatigue, though, when it threatens to eat up my time and my efforts at a good work—when I'm tempted to stay home from church (or with COVID-19, sleep in on a Sunday past the time for virtual church), as examples—I try to remember that we wrestle "not against flesh and blood, but … against the spiritual forces of evil in the heavenly realms" (Ephesians 6:12). For the most part, this causes me to dig into Jesus for the strength to overcome.

Scripture also tells us:

> A little sleep, a little slumber, a little folding of the hands to rest—
> and poverty will come on you like a bandit and scarcity like an
> armed man. (Proverbs 6:10–11; 24:33–34)

My computer is in my bedroom. How often I have been at work and felt my bed calling to me: "Sleep! You need more sleep!" Frequently, I am left with a choice to get "suited up," "stand" (Ephesians 6:13), and stay in the fight, or give in and relent.

Certainly, when I haven't slept well the night before, or an excursion has kept me up late, it's only natural and normal to feel fatigue. In addition, with the aging process, as we get older and find that we cannot do as much as we used to without getting tired, taking a nap is often a great remedy.

Hear me when I say that what I'm referring to is unreasonable fatigue— fatigue for which there is no apparent physical cause or reason. I know that the devil will try his utmost, for instance, to keep me from an intimate relationship with my Savior. Many times, he influenced me to close my eyes and nod off when I was before Jesus for my time of prayer. At such times, I would try to recognize the source of the fatigue and pray that God would help me not to succumb to temptation.

I knew of a great psychologist who would push beyond his fatigue, working long hours under great strain at Lyndhurst, a hospital for people with spinal cord injuries. He was willing to give me an appointment well after his workday was over, without the slightest bit of irritation or impatience, just because I wheeled up to his office and asked him for one. He was a great professional. To me, that was so special, particularly since my parents were unapproachable and highly irritable in my childhood and youth.

> Do everything without grumbling or arguing, so that you may become blameless and pure, "children of God without fault in a warped and crooked generation." Then you will shine among them like stars in the sky as you hold firmly to the word of life. (Philippians 2:14–16a)

This psychologist shone like a "[star] in the sky" to me at that most difficult time of my early years in the chair.

We need to be wise when it comes to fatigue, if we are to consistently accomplish good works. Fatigue, though, can be a gauge—a necessary and helpful one at that. It can be telling us that we are burning the candle at both ends or demanding more of ourselves than is healthy. If this is the case with you, remember Jesus's words—He *promises* rest to all who come to Him (Matthew 11:28–30).

When I was about to complete my studies, I found the last few courses were the most arduous of any in the three years of each degree. Satan tried to keep me from accomplishing and finishing the work to which God had called me. Satan will also stop at nothing to prevent God's people from doing what they need to do to stay close to Jesus. God alone can exchange your heaviness with lightness and joy from His heart to yours. It was Nehemiah who said, "The joy of the Lord is your strength" (8:10). Let His joy that surpasses circumstances lift you up to help you overcome unreasonable fatigue.

CHAPTER TWENTY-NINE

SOME PARTICULARLY HELPFUL SCRIPTURE

*T*here is nothing more powerfully healing than the Holy Spirit interacting with the Word for a born-again believer. Remember my telling you that Joyce Meyer quit her full-time job in order to study the Bible for a full year to prepare herself for her world-wide ministry? You may not be preparing for a world-wide ministry, but you have a ministry in your own life, with the people around you. I pray the Lord speaks to you through this list (certainly not exhaustive) of particularly encouraging and helpful scripture especially for the heavy-hearted. (You may choose to memorize some of these verses to better equip yourself to deal with the enemy.)

> Let us not become weary in doing good, for at the proper time we will reap a harvest if we do not give up. (Galatians 6:9)

> But as for you, be strong and do not give up, for your work will be rewarded. (2 Chronicles 15:7)

> It is written: "I believed; therefore I have spoken." Since we have that same spirit of faith we also believe and therefore speak, because we know that the one who raised the Lord Jesus from the dead will also raise us with Jesus and present us with you to himself. All this is for your benefit, so that the grace that

is reaching more and more people may cause thanksgiving to overflow to the glory of God.

Therefore we do not lose heart. Though outwardly we are wasting away, yet inwardly we are being renewed day by day. For our light and momentary troubles are achieving for us an eternal glory that far outweighs them all. So we fix our eyes not on what is seen, but on what is unseen. For what is seen is temporary, but what is unseen is eternal. (2 Corinthians 4:13–18)

Whoever wants to be my disciple must deny themselves and take up their cross daily and follow me. (Luke 9:23)

Some of the most difficult elements of Christian life—for me, at least—involve laying down self-will, and accepting and embracing my particular, personal truth on a daily basis. Though challenging, the Christian life is one that is meant to be enjoyed. Joyce Meyer has entitled her television program, *Enjoying Everyday Life*. She means that in getting the kids off to school on time, in making the meals, in doing the dishes, we can enjoy our everyday lives. "[We] can do all this through … [Christ] who gives … [us] strength" (Philippians 4:13).

Watch out that you do not lose what we have worked for, but that you may be rewarded fully. (2 John 1:8)

Then Jesus told his disciples a parable to show them that they should always pray and not give up. (Luke 18:1)

What follows this verse is called the Parable of the Persistent Widow. If you'll recall, it's about a woman in need who hounds an unjust judge with her petitions. The judge finally relents, saying to himself,

"Even though I don't fear God or care what people think, yet because this widow keeps bothering me, I will see that she gets justice, so that she won't eventually come and attack me!"

And the Lord said, "Listen to what the unjust judge says. And will not God bring about justice for his chosen ones, who cry out to him day and night? Will he keep putting them off? I tell you, he will see that they get justice, and quickly. However, when the Son of Man comes, will he find faith on the earth?" (Luke 18:4b–8)

You might not see human justice in this realm, but come your judgment day, you surely will, as you hold fast to Jesus.

Be strong and courageous. (Deuteronomy 31:6, 7, 23; Joshua 1:6, 7, 9, 18; 10:25; 1 Chronicles 22:13; 28:20; 2 Chronicles 32:7)

Therefore, I urge you, brothers and sisters, in view of God's mercy, to offer your bodies as a living [*as opposed to dead*] sacrifice, holy and pleasing to God—this is your true and proper worship. Do not conform to the pattern of this world, but be transformed by the renewing of your mind. Then you will be able to test and approve what God's will is—his good, pleasing and perfect will. (Romans 12:1–2)

Do not be overcome by evil, but overcome evil with good. (Romans 12:21)

Keeping God's commands is what counts. (1 Corinthians 7:19, italics mine)

CHAPTER THIRTY

MORE PARTICULARLY HELPFUL SCRIPTURE

EMOTIONS: FEAR, ANGER, ANXIETY

Difficult emotions such as fear, anger or anxiety are feelings with which we all battle. Through Christ and His Word, we can find victory over these troubling emotions.

For God has not given us a spirit of fear, but of power and of love and of a sound mind. (2 Timothy 1:7 NKJV)

Do not fear. (Isaiah 35:4; 41:10, 13; 43:1)

So do not fear, for I am with you; do not be dismayed, for I am your God. I will strengthen you and help you; I will uphold you with my righteous right hand. (Isaiah 41:10)

When I am afraid, I put my trust in you. In God, whose word I praise—in God I trust and am not afraid. What can mere mortals do to me? (Psalm 56:3–4)

The Lord is with me; I will not be afraid. What can mere mortals do to me? The Lord is with me; he is my helper, I look in triumph on my enemies. (Psalm 118:6–7)

Surely God is my salvation; I will trust and not be afraid. The Lord, the Lord himself, is my strength and my defense; he has become my salvation. (Isaiah 12:2)

Don't be afraid; just believe. (Mark 5:36)

Peace I leave with you; my peace I give you. I do not give to you as the world gives. Do not let your hearts be troubled and do not be afraid. (John 14:27)

To fear the Lord is to hate evil; I hate pride and arrogance, evil behavior and perverse speech. (Proverbs 8:13)

"In your anger do not sin:" Do not let the sun go down while you are still angry, and do not give the devil a foothold. (Ephesians 4:26–27)

Cast all your anxiety on him because he cares for you. (1 Peter 5:7)

Do not be anxious about anything, but in every situation, by prayer and petition, with thanksgiving, present your requests to God. And the peace of God, which transcends all understanding, will guard your hearts and your minds in Christ Jesus. (Philippians 4:6–7)

PERSEVERANCE PASSAGES

The Parable of the Sower concludes with these words:

But the seed on good soil stands for those with a noble and good heart, who hear the word, retain it, and by persevering produce a crop. (Luke 8:15)

Other scripture:

If you *hold* to my teaching, you are really my disciples. Then you will know the truth, and the truth will set you free. (John 8:31–32)

[Love] always protects, always trusts, always hopes, always perseveres. (1 Corinthians 13:7)

Note: The above verse does not mean persevering in accepting abuse. If you are experiencing abuse, it's time to learn to set firm boundaries, with God's help.

You need to persevere so that when you have done the will of God, you will receive what he has promised. For,

"In just a little while,
he who is coming will come
and will not delay."

And,

"But my righteous one will live by faith.
And I take no pleasure
in the one who shrinks back."

But we do not belong to those who shrink back and are destroyed, but to those who have faith and are saved. (Hebrews 10:36–39)

Commentaries on this passage say that we need patience and perseverance, that it is through these things that we are able to firmly and constantly advance.

By faith, he [Moses] left Egypt, not fearing the king's anger; he persevered because he saw him who is invisible. (Hebrews 11:27)

Blessed is the one who perseveres under trial because, having stood the test, that person will receive the crown of life that the Lord has promised to those who love him. (James 1:12)

As you know, we count as blessed those who have persevered. You have heard of Job's perseverance and have seen what the Lord finally brought about. The Lord is full of compassion and mercy. (James 5:11)

May the Lord direct your hearts into God's love and Christ's perseverance. (2 Thessalonians 3:5)

I know your deeds, your hard work and your perseverance. (Revelation 2:2a–3)

CHAPTER THIRTY-ONE

EVEN MORE PARTICULARLY HELPFUL SCRIPTURE

Do stick with me with these few chapters on scripture. There is so much healing to be gained from reading, meditating on and memorizing the Word.

FAITHFUL

Know … that the Lord your God is God; he is the faithful God, keeping his covenant of love to a thousand generations of those who love him and keep his commandments. (Deuteronomy 7:9)

To the faithful you [Lord] show yourself faithful, to the blameless you show yourself blameless, to the pure you show yourself pure, but to the devious you show yourself shrewd. (2 Samuel 22:26–27; Psalm 18:25–26)

Love the Lord, all his faithful people! The Lord preserves those who are true to him, but the proud he pays back in full. Be strong and take heart, all you who hope in the Lord. (Psalm 31:23–24)

For the word of the Lord is right and true; he is faithful in all he does. (Psalm 33:4)

The Lord is trustworthy in all he promises and faithful in all he does. (Psalm 145:13b)

He holds success in store for the upright, he is a shield to those whose walk is blameless, for he guards the course of the just and protects the way of his faithful ones. (Proverbs 2:7–8)

We do so desire to hear an acknowledgment of *our* faithfulness over the span of our lives from the Lord with these few but powerful words found in Matthew 25:21 and 25:23, "Well done, good and faithful servant!"

Be joyful in hope, patient in affliction, faithful in prayer. (Romans 12:12)

He will also keep you firm to the end, so that you will be blameless on the day of our Lord Jesus Christ. God is faithful, who has called you into fellowship with his Son, Jesus Christ our Lord. (1 Corinthians 1:8–9)

The one who calls you is faithful, and he will do it. (1 Thessalonians 5:24)

But the Lord is faithful, and he will strengthen and protect you from the evil one. (2 Thessalonians 3:3)

But Christ is faithful as the Son over God's house. And we are his house, if indeed we hold firmly to our confidence and the hope in which we glory. (Hebrews 3:6)

Let us hold unswervingly to the hope we profess, for he who promised is faithful. And let us consider how we may spur one another on toward love and good deeds. (Hebrews 10:23–24)

Be alert and of sober mind. Your enemy the devil prowls around like a roaring lion looking for someone to devour. Resist him, standing firm in the faith, because you know that the family of believers throughout the world is undergoing the same kind of sufferings. (1 Peter 5:8–9)

Be faithful until death, and I will give you the crown of life. (Revelation 2:10c NKJV)

REWARDS

The Lord rewards everyone for their righteousness and faithfulness. (1 Samuel 26:23)

By them [the ordinances of the Lord] your servant is warned; in keeping them there is great reward. (Psalm 19:11)

One thing God has spoken, two things I have heard: "Power belongs to you, God, and with you, Lord, is unfailing love"; and, "You reward everyone according to what they have done." (Psalm 62:11–12)

A wicked person earns deceptive wages, but the one who sows righteousness reaps a sure reward. (Proverbs 11:18)

If your enemy is hungry, give him food to eat; if he is thirsty, give him water to drink. In doing this, you will heap burning coals on his head, and the Lord will reward you. (Proverbs 25:21–22)

I the Lord search the heart and examine the mind, to reward each person according to their conduct, according to what their deeds deserve. (Jeremiah 17:10)

Your eyes are open to the ways of all mankind; you reward each person according to their conduct and as their deeds deserve. (Jeremiah 32:19b)

Blessed are you when people insult you, persecute you and falsely say all kinds of evil against you because of me. Rejoice and be glad, because great is your reward in heaven, for in the same way they persecuted the prophets who were before you. (Matthew 5:11–12)

For the Son of Man is going to come in his Father's glory with his angels, and then he will reward each person according to what they have done. (Matthew 16:27)

But love your enemies, do good to them, and lend to them without expecting to get anything back. Then your reward will be great. (Luke 6:35)

Serve wholeheartedly, as if you were serving the Lord, not people, because you know that the Lord will reward each one for whatever good they do, whether they are slave or free. (Ephesians 6:7–8)

Whatever you do, work at it with all your heart, as working for the Lord, not for human masters, since you know that you will receive an inheritance from the Lord as a reward. It is the Lord Christ you are serving. (Colossians 3:23–24)

Look, I am coming soon! My reward is with me, and I will give to each person according to what they have done. (Revelation 22:12)

CHAPTER THIRTY-TWO

YET AGAIN, MORE HELPFUL SCRIPTURE

WAITING SCRIPTURES

I remain confident of this: I will see the goodness of the Lord in the land of the living. Wait for the Lord; be strong and take heart and wait for the Lord. (Psalm 27:13–14)

I waited patiently for the Lord; he turned to me and heard my cry. He lifted me out of the slimy pit, out of the mud and mire; he set my feet on a rock and gave me a firm place to stand. (Psalm 40:1–2)

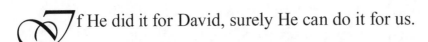

If He did it for David, surely He can do it for us.

I wait for the Lord, my whole being waits, and in his word I put my hope. (Psalm 130:5)

Yet the Lord longs to be gracious to you; therefore he will rise up to show you compassion. For the Lord is a God of justice. Blessed are all who wait for him! (Isaiah 30:18)

Since ancient times no one has heard, no ear has perceived, no eye has seen any God besides you, who acts on behalf of those who wait for him. (Isaiah 64:4)

Wait for the gift my Father promised. (Acts 1:4)

The scriptures speak of "patient endurance" in 2 Corinthians 1:6 and Revelation 1:9; 13:10; and 14:12.

We know that the whole creation has been groaning as in the pains of childbirth right up to the present time. Not only so, but we ourselves, who have the firstfruits of the Spirit, groan inwardly as we wait eagerly for our adoption to sonship, the redemption of our bodies. For in this hope we were saved. But hope that is seen is no hope at all. Who hopes for what they already have? But if we hope for what we do not yet have, we wait for it patiently. (Romans 8:22–25)

ON WAITING

While the Second Coming of Christ is certain:

But about that day or hour no one knows, not even the angels in heaven, nor the Son, but only the Father … Therefore keep watch, because you do not know on what day your Lord will come. But understand this: If the owner of the house had known at what time of night the thief was coming, he would have kept watch and would not have let his house be broken into. So you also must be ready, because the Son of Man will come at an hour when you do not expect him. (Matthew 24:36, 42–44)

Notice Matthew uses the words "must be ready," not you *ought to be ready* or you *should be ready*; it's you *must be ready*. I keep the reality of the return of Christ in the back of my mind, knowing that at any time, I could be relieved of my cross and be taken up with Him. This encourages me to live in a godly fashion that I hope is pleasing to the Lord. It also gives me hope and strength to continue to press on.

Paul speaks of the Second Coming:

> For the grace of God has appeared that offers salvation to all people. It teaches us to say "No" to ungodliness and worldly passions, and to live self-controlled, upright and godly lives in this present age, while we wait for the blessed hope—the appearing of the glory of our great God and Savior, Jesus Christ, who gave himself for us to redeem us from all wickedness and to purify for himself a people that are his very own, eager to do what is good. (Titus 2:11–14)

God's grace instructs us how to live lives that glorify the Savior as we wait for His return. Especially in times of hardship, we need to wait on Him, allowing God to remind us of all the times He has helped us in the past. In hindsight, His blessings are many—a bed to sleep on, a home to rest in, a vehicle to get us around, food in our stomachs, a friend to talk to. Do we tend to take such simple things for granted? Before you start to writhe in frustration because things are not going as you had hoped, wait on God. Ask Him to speak to you. He merely calls you to trust Him, to bring Him your frustration and watch as He melts it away in the peace of His loving presence.

CHAPTER THIRTY-THREE
SELF-ESTEEM

*H*aving healthy self-esteem is very precious. It helps us perform well and do tasks in such a way that our superiors are pleased. Our parents can weave it into us, or contrarily, they can shatter it. It's very difficult to totally counter the effects of an upbringing that held much turmoil. Just as the original sin of one man had such a pervasive and devastating effect on humanity, so the mistreatment of a child can damage and scar that person, to some degree, for life.

Some parents are sensitive and mature, and are able to meet their children's needs of affirmation and encouragement, as well as applying firm discipline when it is required. These children grow to develop healthy boundaries and learn to keep themselves safe. Parents of such children can help their little ones understand God's love for them by modeling it and speaking of it regularly.

Other parents find it hard to cope with the day-to-day struggle of raising a family and find themselves inadvertently lashing out, verbally or perhaps physically, at their children. Later, when life circumstances heat up and things get very tough, adults who were abused in their childhood may have great difficulty withstanding the stress of life because their emotional and spiritual foundations are not strong. Such people may spiral into negativity, something that is only natural, given the childhood abuse. That's why I talk about a predisposition to suicide.

SUICIDAL PREDISPOSITION

It's a curious phenomenon that a certain stressful situation pushes one person past the brink of despair and to contemplate suicide, whereas another person, undergoing the same or similar stress, is able to persevere, perhaps without such thoughts at all.

Grief and despair hit all of us at one time or another. Various factors can push someone over the edge and into entertaining thoughts of suicide, such as abuse, the presence of mental illness (including the lack of the appropriate medication) or addictions, the tendency to catastrophize, a sudden and severe loss, or a weak support network.

Just as Jesus had His disciples, so we all need the support of others. It's up to us to find it, especially if the family to which we belong is unable to give us what we need, emotionally, physically, and/or spiritually. I've heard it said that friends are the family we get to choose. When I became a Christian at age twenty-three and, little by little, experienced the joy of the Lord, Jesus lifted me. As I grew more accustomed to having His joy in my life, I leaned more and more on Christ and spent less time in negativity and sadness. As I allowed Christ to permeate my spirit, I found that others were attracted to that joy, and it was easier to build a healthy social network for myself. As we build trust on both the vertical and horizontal plains, we can keep from acting on the tendencies toward suicidal ideation, something we will face if we suffer from a suicidal predisposition—something I believe is real.

Fundamentally, though, a remedy for suicidal ideation—other than a biochemical solution in the form of psychiatric meds—is the ability to trust and seek God. Although suicidal ideation *is* a symptom of mental illness, suicidal thoughts originate from Satan, as I've repeatedly said for emphasis. Jesus is the Prince of Peace. He conquered the devil, once and for all, with His resurrection. We need to reach to Jesus and surrender our hearts, lives, and trials to Him, and He will bring us through.

Christian recording artist Larnelle Harris sings a song called "The Strength of the Lord." The chorus says that it's not in trying but in trusting. It's not in running but in resting. It's not in wondering but in praying that we find the strength of the Lord. When we try, when we run, and when we wonder, we exert our own strength. When we trust in Him, we look to His divine resources. When we rest in faith, He carries us. When we pray, we find intimacy with and comfort from the Almighty.

The enemy tries to turn us away from God by getting us to place our gaze on our circumstances, instead of on our Creator. As we fix our eyes on God, our circumstances diminish, and He increases. He is an ever-present source of strength, hope, joy, and peace. When the devil comes knocking, we need to lean even more on our beloved Savior, who gives us the strength we need when we trust and seek Him with all our hearts—not striving but taking on His easy yoke (Matthew 11:30).

When I was living in the institution and was mistreated by staff on whom I needed to rely, it came to me that I was not in the hands of anyone but the almighty God. I truly needed to believe Romans 8:28. In doing so, I realized that I had nothing to fear. Not even despair itself—something I felt much of the time when I was in that place—was reason to fear. All God was asking of me was my trust.

Individuals may be prone to developing a suicidal predisposition if they have suffered severe trauma, whether from an accident or abuse of any kind, from childhood or from within an ongoing relationship; did not experience the strengths and joys of a functional family unit; and/or were unable to have a healthy dependence and bonding with their parents in their early years. All these factors can contribute to laying a template of mistrust and fear that may make a person more prone to negativity. In periods of deep distress, that person may almost immediately think of exiting from this world; it can become like a knee-jerk reaction.

However—and this is a big *however*—we need to fully grasp the fundamental truth of Ephesians 6:12: that we are in a spiritual war. Without a clear recognition of the voice of the enemy, anyone is extremely vulnerable and may find it difficult to dispel the thoughts of suicide that Satan ultimately plants in our minds. The unseen realm influences us all day, every day.

I think of the story of Job, in which the devil had to get permission from God at every level of testing of Job (Job 1:9–12; 2:4–6). If you are currently wrestling with suicidal thoughts, to the point where you believe you may have a suicidal predisposition, know that God is sovereign. As a reminder, Dr. Charles Stanley says, nothing happens outside of God's permissive will. God allows those thoughts for a reason. Fear not, and let them come and go.

Rick Warren says in his book, *The Purpose Driven Life,* that character is both developed and revealed by tests; in fact, all life is a test. He says that we are always being tested. God constantly watches our responses to people, problems, success, conflict, illness, disappointment, and even the weather.

Those with a suicidal predisposition are especially prone to testing from the enemy. If this is you, be strong, and cling with all your might to Jesus, the victor over Satan.

CHAPTER THIRTY-FOUR

MORE ON SUICIDAL PREDISPOSITION

ome individuals can find healing through other means, but only Christ severs the spiritual encumbrances that hinder us at the deepest level. It is through a relationship with Christ alone that our heart-bonds with fear and shame are severed as we seek forgiveness and love from Jesus. He comes in and unites our hearts to God, the Holy Spirit. And it's a soul-tie that absolutely nothing can eradicate, says Dr. Charles Stanley.

Conversion is essential, but it is also important to be discipled—to have those who are more mature in the faith help to guide and teach new Christians the basic biblical doctrine, as well as how to walk in the Spirit. Only then can we be walking in God's will. It could be that you suffer with suicidal ideation purely because you were not discipled properly. Seeing Jesus in truth is key to living with and finding victory over a suicidal predisposition.

When the heat is on—especially when wars rage within you—a source of comfort may be childhood memories of your parents praying for you and with you; of your parents going to war for your soul, your safety, and your overall well-being. Know that you are blessed if you are able to draw on such memories.

In a divorce, where children are involved, one parent might unwittingly belittle and denigrate the other parent in the presence of the little ones. The children can be exposed to rage or even hatred between the parents. The children then may become withdrawn after witnessing the hostile feelings of one parent for the other. The kids can be caught in the middle, feeling that if they receive and give love to the "hated" parent, they are betraying the other one; a double bind occurs then. Proper bonding with the parents can fail to take place for such children. This can contribute to the creation of a dependent personality. Unmet dependency needs in childhood can leave those children clinging in desperation for support from just about anyone who says hello, and this tendency can carry on into adulthood; it can also result in a suicidal predisposition because often this type of clinginess is met with rejection after rejection.

With allowed and nourished dependence on godly parents, children can grow in security to eventually shift that dependence on their parents to independence and then to dependence on God. This can then lead to healthy interdependence with others, which is what Jesus modeled in the garden of Gethsemane. If you are in your own garden of Gethsemane, with a suicidal predisposition hounding you, you need special care and consideration, not only from health care professionals but also from family and friends. Look to supportive others in interdependence, and above all, to Jesus to find support and healing for your condition. And remember to be patient with yourself. A suicidal predisposition did not happen overnight; it takes time to find the healing necessary to rise above it.

OTHER RISK FACTORS

Those who are highly sensitive and highly intelligent may also be at greater risk for a suicidal predisposition.

Highly sensitive people may be more prone to taking things personally. They may pick up and be affected more deeply by the moods of others and, therefore, can become discouraged and thrown into despair more easily. This can become a pattern and develop into a suicidal predisposition.

Highly intelligent people may tend to think too much or may not be able to rest in faith when answers don't come. They may get caught up in their minds and find it especially difficult to get down to a heart level. They may try to demand answers where only mystery lies, leading to despondency and despair, which can again lead to a pattern of behavior and repetitive suicidal ideation.

> Above all else, guard your heart, for everything you do flows from it. (Proverbs 4:23)

This verse applies to all, but it strikes me that it is especially important for those who are highly sensitive and highly intelligent.

"MY BROTHER'S KEEPER"

After Cain killed his brother Abel, God inquired about Abel's whereabouts. Cain replied, "I don't know … Am I my brother's keeper?" (Genesis 4:9). If we ask that question, in general, I would respond with a hearty *yes*. Let me explain.

As adults, we are responsible for ourselves. It is purely because this can be such a daunting task, especially if we have a number of nagging health issues, that we need to recognize and accept that we need each other, and that we need to watch out for one another. But maybe we feel that the pain in our brother is just too much to bear, as the weight of our already-heavy cross wears us down. Sometimes we think, *I can't help that person. The need is too great. What can one person do?* I'm always amazed that Satan can throw such thoughts and a feeling of heaviness at me, just before I do a good work for God and extend a hand to a vulnerable one.

Particularly as Christians, we need to have our radar up and respond to broken hearts all around us where appropriate, with love. When you see that downtrodden child or adult, reach out, saying something like, "You seem troubled. What's on your mind?" It isn't so difficult to show that one person a touch of grace. You may not be able to solve people's problems, but they may come away sensing deeply that someone cares, that they matter, and that they are not invisible. Don't leave it up to someone else.

Even seemingly small gestures can have a profound impact and be an encounter that individuals will remember for the rest of their lives. A friend once said to me, "People often need so little, but they need that 'so little' so much." Is there a wounded one in your life to whom you can reach out with the love of Jesus? You may be gifted and blessed with the full richness of His divine love. It needs to be spread around! Take the risk and extend a hand. Speak words of kindness, no matter how insignificant they may seem. Reach out—you never know where it will end up.

Use your imagination when reaching out with the love of God. Exercise and demonstrate your faith. Share the love that you have had generously poured into you.

Freely you have received; freely give. (Matthew 10:8b)

You are Jesus's hands, feet, eyes, and mouth. Remember what E. V. Hill said—that you're it. We're it. Jesus is living His life here on earth through you. Take your role as a conduit of Christ's love seriously. You may have more of a role to play than you think.

Remember that you will be held accountable for how you used your gifts and abilities, whether you spread His love or not. Recall Jesus's words: "By this everyone will know that you are my disciples, if you love one another" (John 13:35). Sharing love should be your trademark as a Christian. You may be the closest thing to Christ that some people ever meet.

It is especially important to reach out to those we know are down or discouraged. Truly, no one ever knows what is passing through someone else's mind. With your encouragement, you might be just the ticket to reinforce that person's belief in humanity or faith in Christ, as that person sees the love of Jesus in action; you may even contribute to saving that person's life. Those who have not experienced the relentless nature of ongoing suicidal ideation may find it hard to relate to someone who has contemplated or attempted suicide, and they may not have the foggiest clue how to reach out to such a person. Just be kind, as you would be to anyone. You may never know what a touch of kindness can do. Mother Teresa once said that you never know just how far a simple smile can go.

We need to be ever mindful of our roles as conduits of Christ. We need to stick especially close to those in great pain, whether it's emotional, physical, or spiritual, because these folks are especially vulnerable to the attacks of the enemy. Jesus referred to them as the "least of these" (Matthew 25:40), those in whom Christ's presence is especially strong. Get involved. Individuals' lives—or certainly their quality of life—may depend on your help, advocacy, and/or intervention, and you may be truly blessed because you did. You may help out, only to find that the broken one is ministering to and becoming Jesus for you. Don't just walk on by. We *are* our brother's keeper.

INDIFFERENCE

It has been said that the opposite of love is not hate but indifference. Indifference denies the interconnectedness—the need for interdependence—within humanity. It denies the idea that we all need each other and that we are all in this together. It can stem from sheer emotional and spiritual exhaustion, or it can result from a basic unwillingness to care about fellow human beings. Ultimately, however, it stems from Satan's planting thoughts in our minds that cause us to isolate and judge people, especially people who are hurting. I witness apathy and indifference from some of my caregivers. They're just doing the job for a paycheck. When they put me in deep frustration, I sometimes feel tempted to say to one of them, "Why don't you get a job as a mail carrier or handler or as a UPS worker, instead of working with vulnerable human beings?" I didn't, though.

Do we listen to those whispers of the enemy and disregard those in pain?

Teacher, do you see the despairing and confused child or adolescent? Or have you heard through the grapevine about that coworker who has encountered trouble? Do you fear getting involved? Why not simply ask that person how he or she is feeling? Why not simply reach out and see where God takes the conversation? The hurting one may be in denial and push you away, but more likely, he or she will appreciate your gesture. We all have limits and can only give so much, but remember that "people often need so little, but they need that 'so little' so much!"

Sometimes Satan plants thoughts in our minds like, *It won't matter*, or *It'll make little difference to reach out*. Be aware of his subtle influence, and reach out anyway. You never know what it will accomplish. It may lead to your sharing your faith! Who knows where any of us would be today, if not for this disease called indifference?

CHAPTER THIRTY-FIVE

IN RUIN

$\mathcal{G}$od can choose not to intervene, and our lives can come to ruin.

> This is what the Sovereign Lord says: … "A ruin! A ruin! I will make it a ruin!" (Ezekiel 21:26a–27a)

Perhaps this describes your life right now. When I was newly injured with the spinal cord injury, I felt abject hatred and disdain for life. Three years previous to this, I was flying high, celebrating the graduation of my master's degree with family and friends. Especially when I was forced to go and live in an institution, I was livid and I made this known to God in no uncertain terms. I had had a difficult beginning and now God was asking me to spend the rest of my life in a wheelchair? I was mad, to say the least!!

As a reminder, it took about three years but Jesus transformed me, ultimately using my church—the body of believers—and my family, from whom, in particular, I found practical love and acceptance at the time.

Jill Phillips sings a song that says, "Triumph and tragedy, only God can be both the builder and the wrecking ball." Certainly, in our finite understanding, we can see Him as one or the other. Remember, however, my favorite verse—that God's ways are not our ways. What you see as ruinous, God may view in another way.

By the world's standards, Jesus's life on earth came to ruin. He was brutally beaten and left to die on a Roman cross between two thieves. Although Jesus had told the disciples that He would rise again, they may have been tempted to discouragement and despair between the time of Christ's death and His resurrection. And, as you know, Jesus's dying on that cross was the Father's will for His beloved Son! As we look with spiritual eyes, oh, what spiritual riches—your eternal salvation and mine—was won on that cross from the situation that was ruinous, by all worldly standards.

If you feel that all about you is in ruin, just watch, wait, trust, and see what God can do. Don't give up hope. God is definitely a God who loves to tackle and resolve impossible situations. Remember, "all things are possible with God" (Mark 10:27).

SUFFERING QUIETLY

God calls us to share in Jesus's sufferings, and I believe that He is looking for people to do it quietly—quietly but not silently. Of course, you need discernment when sharing your story, but don't hide yourself away. Tell your story when you choose and with whomever you can trust, but don't do it with an angry or a complaining spirit. I believe that displeases the Lord. Do it quietly; don't be shy to let people know. Remember that Paul boasted in his sufferings (see 2 Corinthians 11:23–28). It may not only be an incredible source of healing for you, but it can also motivate and uplift others to hear what God is doing in your life.

People need to hear about your suffering so they know how to pray and so they can get a before-and-after picture. God can bless people who can articulate what they are going through. It can provide clarity, insight, and perspective to the sufferer, as well as to teach and inspire others, giving them insight into the work of God. Share your suffering, but do it quietly.

ON BULLIES

Maybe your suffering includes someone or some people in your life who are bullies. As the family scapegoat, my entire family ganged up on me, especially when I was little. I also encountered bullies in the institution—nurses who could do only the basic physical tasks and who chose to push their weight around. My only recourse was to respond to these people by not taking it personally. (Certainly as a child, I did not have this option, but as an adult, I did.) I understood that they were demonstrating their own insecurities by trying to control through anger, fear, and hurt. I knew that they did not cope well with their own vulnerability.

Many bullies need to control through hurting others because of their own deep-seated fears. They may have been bullied in their lives, particularly in childhood, and they learned to approach the vulnerable by attempting to squash their spirits, as perhaps was done to them. As a reminder, my mother was a scapegoat in her family of origin, and she inadvertently passed this on.

I found it powerful and helpful to pray for bullies. After all, we are called to "love our enemies and pray for those who persecute [us]" (Matthew 5:44). This would free me to "love the sinner but hate the sin." It gave me the ability to separate the two. If you find yourself the victim of bullying, pray for those who treat you as such, wait and watch to see what God will do.

"HAVEN'T I SUFFERED ENOUGH?"

Maybe you've asked God, "Have I suffered enough?" Somehow, you sense that you want or expect things to go your way, and when they don't, you are disappointed, or perhaps devastated. Having suffered enough, as you may believe, you may feel you deserve a break and for things to go well. You think that somehow, since you've suffered for God and endured, you should have earned favor with God. Perhaps you believe that He ought to be lenient with you, but you were left in confusion and bewilderment when hard times hit again.

Suffering is no respecter of persons; even it seems that God heaps it on those especially close to Him as a way to make them more like Him. Joni Eareckson Tada says that Jesus puts suffering between you and Him so that there will be nothing between you and Him.

Certainly, Paul suffered enormously (see 2 Corinthians11:23–28). Yet, Paul ended up writing some of the greatest words ever penned because he endured. Indeed, although He was innocent, Jesus had to suffer willingly and in the most excruciating way for us to have the Savior of the world. Don't give up; there are reasons why you are here, and there are reasons why you are to go on.

Someone once said that we do not come to God because things are going so well that we want someone to thank. It is through suffering that He draws us to Him. I was in a deep, dark pit of depression when God wooed me with butterflies, around the time of my conversion. God used that suffering to draw me to Him and seal my eternal destiny for all time.

Take your frustrations and your questions about your suffering to Him, and let Him decide when you have suffered enough. One day, all will be explained; we will know all. Be patient and wait for that day. Wait for His timing. Time moves at a steady and quick pace; it'll come faster than you think.

FREEDOM THROUGH HARD TIMES

I truly believe there is freedom to be found through deep suffering.

I went sailing with a volunteer several years after I had the spinal cord injury. In speaking with him while on the open water, I said that I'd eventually found enormous freedom after having the injury that put me in a wheelchair. Through the darkness of that time, I acquired a freedom from things—a freedom from idolatry, including idolatry of my home. I had watched TV news reports of homes going up in flames and thought to myself that even homes are expendable. This became even more real to me when I was forced to relinquish the apartment I'd had as an able-bodied person—the one that had come fully furnished, the one I had lived in for over ten years—to live in an institution. We ought not put our faith in our homes but in Christ alone.

Jesus says to the rich young man, "Go, sell everything you have and give to the poor, and you will have treasure in heaven. Then come, follow me" (Mark 10:21). Jesus taught me, some time after getting into the chair, not to put my hope into temporal, earthly things because I can't take them with me. While I need things, God tells me not to spiritually rely on them, as that is idolatry (Exodus 20:4; Deuteronomy 5:8). After all, everything can break down and become useless. Be reminded that only Christlikeness—that which we do in Christ's service and which is honed in our character through suffering, for example—is of eternal value.

Now I'm much more appreciative, in general, of that which I used to take for granted. I now thank God for a roof over my head. I thank God for food in my stomach. I thank God for the gifts, talents, and abilities He has graciously given me. In the institution, I met people like Paul Capon, now in glory, who used a device with a keyboard in order to "talk." He had great patience in typing out every letter of everything he wanted to "say," and the computer would "speak" for him. Mr. Capon was happy to communicate with anyone who took the time to do so. Observing folks like Mr. Capon made me more appreciative of that which I had previously taken for granted, like my voice. The ability to readily verbalize is something so important to me particularly as a woman; I cannot imagine being without it.

Now, I try to think of everything as a blessing from God. I thank Him for the relatives and friends who love and relate to me. I thank Him for the sunshine, for radiant flowers that delight, for all creation. I work hard to incorporate 1 Thessalonians 5:18 into my daily life.

I value my relationship with Christ above all, including the heart-to-heart conversations I have with Him. I value these with people as well. I value what I call love moments—moments of tenderness between me and my loved ones and between me and my caregivers. When my father died, I struggled emotionally. During that time, my caregiver highlighted my need for the hospital, really acting as my advocate and encouraging me to reach out for help, as the biochemical imbalance in my brain, my depression, had reared its ugly head. She cared enough to comment and not just ignore my condition, as many of my other caregivers would have chosen to do. Her advocacy was indeed a love moment.

Years after my spinal cord injury, I would often offer words of comfort to a fellow traveler who was in a deep place. This person sensed that my Christ could actually reach him in his space and could bring not only comfort (2 Corinthians 1:3–7) but salvation.

Paul said,

> To the weak, I became weak, to win the weak. I have become all things to all people so that by all possible means I might save some. (1 Corinthians 9:22)

Jesus put me in a vulnerable position so that I might reach others who also are vulnerable. Trust that Jesus is doing something beautiful spiritually in and through your deep suffering.

The truth will set you free. (John 8:32)

Embrace the truth about your painful situation and you too will find that freedom you crave, though this may be an eventual process.

CHAPTER THIRTY-SIX
PLEASURE IN ILLNESS

There is a strange phenomenon where one can actually feel pleasure in illness. Perhaps it's the extra attention or the chance to rest—to escape into sleep and a comfy, warm bed. Or perhaps it's that people who normally are not that pleasant become kind to you when something is wrong with you.

When I was a child, my mother was much more attentive to me whenever I was ill than at other times. This is normally the case for any mother and child, but for me, it was extra special because, as a reminder, my mom was virtually unapproachable in general. She would most often snap at me or dismiss me if I reached out to her when I was little. She felt so very stressed. Mind you, raising three small children by yourself, as she did, certainly is no easy task, even for the healthiest of moms.

Our loving heavenly Father loves us no matter what the circumstances, but when I am ill, I tend to think more about Him. I draw near to Him, and I feel Him drawing near to me. If you have a serious illness, draw near to Him. He is calling you to this through the pain. He is, after all, the Great Physician who has the ability to heal your body and your emotions, if and when He so chooses.

You may not be able to make sense of your suffering or why God is allowing it, especially if your condition is deteriorating. I firmly believe that God allows deep pain in our lives so we can learn to lean on Him in this life, as a dry run for how we will relate to Him in the hereafter. Trust that there is a purpose. Even those barely alive can draw compassion and gratitude from those who interact with the severely broken one. When we see someone who is very debilitated, we can be drawn to the ill one in community and to God in prayer. There is a spiritual richness to those who are very incapacitated. There is great meaning and purpose in the intense suffering. Indeed, God resides in such as these (Matthew 25:40) and has special insight and blessings to shower on these persons and on those who love them.

Getting back to you and your illness, it can draw kindness and compassion from those around you. It can have a positive effect on others who witness your pain when they see you handle it with God's grace. Certainly, God has great compassion for you in your pain. I pray that He brings others to minister to you and to provide comfort if this describes you, as Job's friends did for him, well, sort of; certainly, they listened to him. However, they did, as well, suggest that what happened to him was a result of some kind of sin in his life (e.g., Job 4:7; 8:20; 11:13–15).

Recall that aside from letting Job have his say and hearing him out, they did do one really good thing: "Then they sat on the ground with him for seven days and seven nights. No one said a word to him, because they saw how great his suffering was" (Job 2:13).

If your suffering is so great you have no words, maybe you can sense the presence of Christ in your room. Rest in faith, friend, knowing that He has things in His control and that He is working out His purposes in and through you as you submit and surrender your suffering to Him.

Know that Jesus wants to sit with you and use this time to show you how very special you are. He wants to fill you and others with His Spirit. And it's not wrong if you experience some pleasure in your illness. Just keep reaching out and looking up. May you find not only kind horizontal attention from those around you especially if you are not well, but divine, vertical care from the Holy Trinity.

TAKE UP YOUR CROSS

As we take up our crosses, we can look to God, as well as to scripture, for help. The Bible was created to give us strength to bear our crosses, to keep on, and to endure. It's one big encouragement book. It was written to advise and to guide us how to proceed, not to *recede*. Jesus speaks openly of our need to deny ourselves as well, saying, "If anyone would come after me, he must deny himself and take up his cross and follow me" (Matthew 16:24; Mark 8:34). Notice here that Jesus uses the word *must*. Denying yourself or putting yourself to death can be a very painful process. Suicide is not denying self; it is indulging self. For some, it could be seen as the ultimate act of hedonism. You may believe that you would be instantly transported to a pain-free, blissful existence alongside your Savior. And that may very well be what would happen if you were to take that most drastic step, but it is about pride and feelings. It is about a selfish, narrow viewpoint that you need to be rid of your pain. It's a way of saying, "This pain is purposeless, and I'd be better off without it," neither of which I believe is true. And it's a way of saying to God, "I know best, and I want to do this." Again, it is not denying self but indulging it. It is indulging feelings. It is not following Jesus's example when He said, "Not as I will, but as You will" (Matthew 26:39).

We can find victory by keeping our eyes fixed on Jesus to find the strength to wrestle with difficult feelings, one at a time. Keeping our eyes on what we *feel* only intensifies the pain. Life is not about feelings. We all have good days and bad days, in terms of feelings. On the good days, rejoice in the blessings God bestows upon you. On the bad days, we need to cling with desperation to Jesus for strength and courage to see us through until the bad days pass. Don't act out on a bad day by giving in to suicidal thoughts.

Times will come when we will be especially tempted to discouragement and despair, when we will feel our fragility and vulnerability more intensely. With COVID-19, for example, our frail health is highlighted. It is especially in times like these that we need to stay close to the Savior and to scriptural truth. Remember His promise to complete the good work He began in you (Philippians 1:6). Remember this, especially, if you feel fed up with life and are about to lay down your cross.

PAUL ON DEPARTING

Paul knew the temptation of laying down his cross. He writes,

> For to me, to live is Christ and to die is gain.

> If I am to go on living in the body, this will mean fruitful labor for me. Yet what shall I choose? I do not know! I am torn between the two: I desire to depart and be with Christ, which is better by far; but it is more necessary for you that I remain in the body.

> Convinced of this, I know that I will remain, and I will continue with all of you for your progress and joy in the faith, so that through my being with you again your boasting in Christ Jesus will abound on account of me. (Philippians 1:21–26)

Paul knew what it was to want to be with Jesus. He knew profound suffering (see 2 Corinthians 11:23–28). And he came to the conclusion that he needed to remain on earth for the sake of others. He understood that people would be hurt and grieved if he were to depart and perhaps take his death into his own hands. Others gain inspiration and hope and, as Paul writes here, their boasting in Jesus will flourish in seeing him press on. If you feel like giving up, know that your movement forward, no matter how incremental and small, can bless God and give encouragement to those around you, whereas your suicide would possibly devastate many.

TREASURES IN HEAVEN

In moving forward, we can build up treasures. Jesus says,

> Do not lay up for yourselves treasures on earth, where moth and rust destroy and where thieves break in and steal; but lay up for yourselves treasures in heaven, where neither moth nor rust destroys, and where thieves do not break in and steal.
>
> For where your treasure is, there your heart will be also. (Matthew 6:19–21 NKJV)

Each day, we have the opportunity to gather more treasures in heaven. Each day that we forge on, there are new opportunities to share Christ, to encourage someone, to build someone up, to offer hope, to store up more goodies, so that when our time comes to pass from this earth, we will enjoy our rewards for all eternity.

> Serve wholeheartedly, as if you were serving the Lord, not people, because you know that the Lord will reward each one for whatever good they do, whether they are slave or free. (Ephesians 6:7–8)

It's all built a day at a time, or, as Joyce Meyer says, "little by little." Joni Eareckson Tada says that the Lord gives us enough grace just for the day. It's truly all you need!

CHAPTER THIRTY-SEVEN
VICARIOUS ENJOYMENT

Vicarious enjoyment is particularly for those who are disabled or confined in some way. When a friend or relative comes home after a vacation, others gather around to hear the details and see the photos taken on the trip. The disabled, especially, can take specific pleasure in hearing such stories, as their sources of pleasure are often more limited.

If your pleasures are curtailed, sometimes you need to take stock and find enjoyment elsewhere—in small things, like the laughter of a child, the chirp of a sparrow, or a piece of dark chocolate (yum!). I have been known to enjoy watching people on a roller coaster at a theme park, listening to the screams and hollers as they fly down the steep hills and whistle around the tight corners. Sometimes, just getting out in creation can be difficult, particularly for those in wheelchairs. Hikes are rarely possible. So again, learn to find pleasure in small things, especially if small things are all you have available to you.

ENTERING IN

By entering into the lives of those around you in a polite, friendly, nonintrusive way, you can gain fulfillment and satisfaction. When appropriate, talk to those around you about what they experience, about their reality. For instance, I often attempt to engage the many drivers and attendants I have by asking them how their day is going and/or how they are feeling. I try to meet them at the point where they find themselves. It's what coming alongside is all about.

Some people will not let you in. They put up barriers and answer tersely. Others will engage with you, making that precious human connection (so important, especially with the social isolation of COVID-19).

We all have people in our lives who help us—doctors, nurses, checkout persons in the grocery store. There are those who interact with me in a holistic way and those who merely attend to the physical task. Some see me as a whole person, and others see that part of the person to which they are relating. I notice that those in the former group seem to come and go with smiles on their faces, but for those in the latter group, I feel their sense of tedium and drudgery.

Practice entering into the lives of those around you, and watch as their world—and yours too—blossoms. As it's been said, bloom where you're planted.

PARALYSIS OF THE WILL

I see people everywhere who are disabled, in that they suffer from paralysis of the will. Many of these people live in a state of low-grade depression; they are living what Charles Stanley calls a "settle-for life," going wearily from one day to the next, not willing to resolve the deep issues that weigh them down and often not even realizing or recognizing the problem. They are trying so hard in self-effort that they are exhausted.

Some are blinded by denial and are too strong to be weak. It takes courage to allow yourself to be vulnerable, to acknowledge your own brokenness, to trade dependence on yourself for dependence on God.

Dependence on God is always good, for God is 100 percent trustworthy, unlike any human being. Although what He does and what He allows is sometimes beyond our comprehension, God is faithful. Even "if we are faithless, he [Jesus] is faithful, for he cannot disown himself" (2 Timothy 2:13).

When I was newly injured and forced to live in the institution, I would not have used the adjective *trustworthy* to describe Him at that time. He did, however, as you know, in true Romans 8:28 fashion, slowly turn that tragedy and desperate situation around. God eventually taught me to give thanks for the paraplegia, as it became one of the greatest teaching tools God has used in my life.

God is ultimately the provider of all our needs. He can break us down just to build us up and provide for us on a deeper level than ever before. Though we will suffer, we can, through our utter dependence on God, be free in our spirits and in our will. It is, after all, in our spirits that we soar.

If you think you may be paralyzed in your will, trust God today. Look not to yourself or to others, but wholly and fully lean on Jesus, and watch as He moves you forward, slowly, inch by precious inch.

PLEASURE VERSUS JOY

It strikes me that there is a difference between pleasure and joy. Pleasure is a sensation based on circumstances, whereas the joy of the Lord can be ever-present and can see us through even the darkest of valleys.

Some seem to opt for seeking sensual pleasures, like those involved in premarital sex or fornication, for instance. Paul speaks on this:

> Now to the unmarried and the widows I say: It is good for them to stay unmarried, as I do.

> But if they cannot control themselves, they should marry, for it is better to marry than to burn with passion. (1 Corinthians 7:8–9; see also 1 Corinthians 6:13–16; 7:3–5)

Recall also,

> Put to death, therefore, whatever belongs to your earthly nature:
> sexual immorality, impurity, lust, evil desires and greed, which
> is idolatry. (Colossians 3:5)

Note that the King James Version of the Bible uses "fornication" instead of "sexual immorality" in this verse as well as in Matthew 15:19.

To me, those involved in this type of sin have exchanged pleasure for the joy that God places in our hearts as a result of our obedience to Him.

"Trust and obey, for there's no other way to be happy in Jesus, than to trust and obey," says the song by John H. Sammis. However, that's not so easily done. Consider these additional passages from Paul:

> So I say, walk by the Spirit, and you will not gratify the desires
> of the flesh.
>
> For the flesh desires what is contrary to the Spirit, and the Spirit
> what is contrary to the flesh.
>
> They are in conflict with each other, so that you are not to do
> whatever you want. (Galatians 5:16–17)

Elsewhere in scripture, Paul exclaims, "I do not understand what I do" (Romans 7:15–25). Remember that we are in a fierce battle, not only around us but within us. In light of these last two passages, in particular, be gentle with yourself if you find yourself indulging the flesh. Remember that "our struggle is … against the spiritual forces of evil" (Ephesians 6:10–12). We are not perfect; only Jesus is sinless. We, as humans, are prone to falling.

Recall Jesus's teaching regarding the woman caught in adultery, whom the teachers of the Law and the Pharisees wanted to stone.

> "Let any one of you who is without sin be the first to throw a stone at her."
>
> … At this, those who heard began to go away one at a time, the older ones first, until only Jesus was left, with the woman still standing there. (John 8:7, 9)

Recall as well that Jesus forgave her: "Neither do I condemn you … Go now and leave your life of sin" (John 8:11). Can we receive, as this woman did, Jesus's tenderness and forgiveness when we fall? Use these beautiful qualities of Jesus through genuine repentance as a model to then forgive yourself, if that's what's called for.

Paul describes the "fruit of the Spirit," which is "love, joy, peace, long-suffering, kindness, goodness, faithfulness, gentleness, self-control" (Galatians 5:22–23 NKJV). God actually builds these qualities into the life of a Christian who walks by the Spirit, not indulging in fleshly pleasures but receiving Jesus's strength to live in a godly fashion. Unbelievers can try to display these fruits through self-effort, but it is actually God who produces these qualities as an offshoot of obedience in the lives of devoted Christians. As they faithfully walk in step with the Spirit, surrendering self-will and self-government, giving up control of their lives to God, He rewards them with this delightful "fruit." Whatever benefits or earthly pleasures people may reap by indulging in the sinful or earthly nature, the opportunity to have the fruit of the Spirit in their lives is well worth the "sacrifice" they may initially feel they make to give up worldly ways.

> He [Moses] chose to be mistreated along with the people of God rather than to enjoy the fleeting pleasures of sin.
>
> He regarded disgrace for the sake of Christ as of greater value than the treasures of Egypt, because he was looking ahead to his reward. (Hebrews 11:25–26)

Can we, like Moses, choose to set aside "the fleeting pleasures of sin" so we can have the reward of God's fruit for now and into eternity?

For your friends or relatives who believe that life is good without God, let me tell you that living in the power of the Holy Spirit is better than any ecstasy the world has to offer. To feel God interacting with me through song, through written or spoken word, through people, or through His Word—to actually sense the supernatural—is life at its finest. There is a song by Salvador that says, "Can you feel the supernatural, the way He wants to love?" Live close to God, and you will feel it too.

CHAPTER THIRTY-EIGHT

A SADDER PLACE

At some point, a person's thoughts can turn toward heaven, even toward ending his or her life. I understand how strongly Satan can push such people into believing that it's the best thing for them to die.

If you have ever felt like checking out of life, I'm here to say that it would be a sadder place without you. There would be an empty space where you were—a lonely, empty space where your warm, beating-heart body was—for all eternity. You would be missed. The contribution you were intended to make in this world would be forever lost. It would be a sadder place without you. Forever. For sure.

MUD OR STARS?

A change in perspective can be so helpful.

When life leads us to ponder death and the afterlife, it is possible to dwell on thoughts of death or even to receive comfort from them. These thoughts can provide an escape from a world we may experience as harsh, cold, cruel, and excruciating.

Especially for those who suffered from anxiety and depression as children, who spent much time in the black, the world may be seen as *not* a loving, protective place but as a hostile one—one in which those children may have even felt they did not belong. Such feelings can carry on into adulthood.

With these adults in particular, thoughts of suicide may encourage the already-present degree of depression and may act almost like comfort food for the mind. Such people are at home in the depths, and thoughts of ending their lives can become like the "candy of despair." For some, depression may be such familiar territory that they might allow themselves to revel in thoughts and plans of suicide, as if they were enjoying a hard candy.

Dwelling on thoughts of suicide, however, is tantamount to entertaining the devil. He can use such thoughts to exhaust you and to reinforce hopelessness. With life being as tough as it is, don't be surprised if Satan hurls such thoughts into your mind at some point in your life, if he hasn't already. When these thoughts come, though, know that you need to dismiss them and lay them aside. Again, dwelling on these thoughts is leaning into Satan. Still, you can overcome a tendency to dwell on suicidal ideation by offering everything and anything up in prayer and finding things, however small, for which to give God thanks (barring the presence of psychosis, of course).

Suicidal ideation is a staring down, whereas prayer is a looking up. Oscar Wilde once said, "Two men look out a window. One sees mud, the other sees the stars." If you are despairing, can you get your gaze off your circumstances, out of the black, and look into the eyes of the Savior, who is hope personified? Can you lay your heart bare before Him, as He made Himself so vulnerable for you by allowing Himself to be beaten, mocked, ridiculed, and crucified on a cruel Roman cross? If your reality is cruel, can you remember what He suffered just for you?

> Let us run with endurance the race marked out for us, looking unto Jesus, the author and finisher of our faith, who for the joy set before Him endured the cross, despising the shame, and has sat down at the right hand of the throne of God. (Hebrews 12:1–2 NKJV)

We can all find great comfort in pouring out our hearts to Jesus and in listening to His reply. Truly, that dialogue is why life is worth living, at least for me.

When Adam and Eve sinned, we were put in a prison of sorts, and we will stay there, as long as we are in these bodies. But thank God for Jesus, who built stars not only that we can see but to which one day we will go—because of His courage, because of His substitutionary death.

ELLEN'S RECIPE FOR LIFE

I have a personal recipe for a healthy life, made up of certain practices:

- heavy daily doses of scripture, plus journaling as you go
- deep and courageous daily heart-to-heart dialogue with God in prayer and in fellowship with others
- regular but nonintrusive entering into the lives of those around you
- disciplined walks of thirty minutes daily (or nearly daily)
- disciplined work, preferably in an area that uses your gifts
- weekly fun, down time for you and Jesus, with your family and/or friends

CHAPTER THIRTY-NINE
MY SELFISH NEED

As I've said, at some point in just about every adult life, suicidal thoughts may cross our minds. That might be you at this moment. Forgive me, but I have a selfish need to have you around. You may even feel Satan's relentless attacks through regular suicidal ideation, with thoughts of ending your life engulfing you this very day. Maybe you find yourself driven by thoughts of harming yourself, and you fantasize about an end to the pain—a blissful release into the arms of Jesus.

If the Father had intended for Jesus to die earlier than he did and in another way, the Father certainly could have accomplished that. He had a purpose in Jesus's suffering—in the beatings, the mockery, and the cross—that are His and His alone. The Father chose to fulfill His purpose through Jesus's suffering. So it is with our suffering. Of course, we are not Christ, but suffering has a redemptive quality to it nonetheless, as we surrender it to Him. He is fulfilling His purpose for us through our suffering, something He may only reveal to us when we meet Him on our judgment day. We need to trust, have faith, and wait.

Jesus knew pain of every sort:

> He was despised and rejected by mankind, a man of suffering and familiar with pain. (Isaiah 53:3)

You may be in relentless agony. So was the case with Jesus. Recall His words in Gethsemane: "My soul is overwhelmed with sorrow to the point of death" (Matthew 26:38). And yet, He went on. Can we follow the example Jesus gave us by pressing on until the Father sets the time to take us home?

Does it seem selfish to you that I want you to go on, despite your great suffering, for the sake of my well-being? You might think so if you are in extreme anguish. I say again, however: I want to have you around. I want you to go on so that I won't have the feelings that will come if you go before your (His) time—guilt, anger, sorrow. As well, I need another human role model, other than Jesus, of how someone with intense suffering endures. I need a model of another person with a strong faith who trusts in God under the most difficult of circumstances.

A song says, "I'm tired of living, but I'm afraid to die." If you too feel this way, get connected; get plugged in to the power source, Jesus Christ, in a big way to help you overcome that fatigue. There's another song: "Because He lives, I can face tomorrow. Because He lives, all fear is gone." Jesus lives within us as born-again believers, and this eradicates the fear of death because we can be assured of a place in heaven when we die. We can then learn to let Him lead, allowing Him to dictate and live out His will for our lives. He would never command you to destroy yourself (or endorse it). Again, that temptation does not come from God. Remember Jesus's words (a good verse to put to memory): "The thief comes only to steal and kill and destroy; I have come that they may have life, and have it to the full" (John 10:10). This verse is one of my very favorites because it is so the truth. I have gone from believing my life was over after a spinal cord injury to going on three separate cruises, living it up like I had never done as an able-bodied person! Believe that Jesus can bring you out of your current pain or grief, if that is you, to soar once again!

Satan can influence the heart that is "deceitful above all things" (Jeremiah 17:9), by gaining entry into your mind with suicidal thoughts. And with those thoughts, he creates despair. He will then try to use those feelings of despair, on top of the natural wickedness of the human heart, to overwhelm and engulf you.

Imagine how many people lost their lives in natural disasters who were not ready to die. Imagine the folks who were diagnosed with terminal illnesses when life was previously good. Imagine all those who succeeded in taking their lives, only to feel deep, profound, and irreversible regret when they got to the other side. Imagine all those who attempted suicide, survived and later told of how grateful they were that they did not succeed (like me!).

God has gifted you with your various abilities. If you find yourself almost overcome with despair, reach into yourself and imagine what life would be like without your God-given abilities. Do the work of entering into the world of those less fortunate than you, those who live daily in a compromised physical, developmental, or emotional state. It will give you a greater appreciation for your own life, and put a different spin on your own suffering.

You have a resilient spirit, more resilient than you know. Often, the most difficult time is the onset of the painful experience. As you know, following my spinal cord injury, I was deeply suicidal—for years. But slowly, over time, God brought me out of it. He can do it for you as well. As you patiently endure, your spirit too can adjust to *your* circumstances.

What if Job had committed suicide? He would not have been able to enjoy the blessings that God bestowed on him after his time of suffering was over. More important, Job would not have understood or had the insights into God that he had if he had not endured his suffering. After speaking to his "comforters" and to the Lord Himself, Job said,

> Surely I spoke of things I did not understand, things too wonderful for me to know … My ears had heard of you but now my eyes have seen you. Therefore I despise myself and repent in dust and ashes. (Job 42:3b, 5–6)

Seems Job had regret for speaking as he had about and to God. Will you one day feel regret over attitudes and beliefs you held about God?

Whether you feel it or not, you are needed in the intricate tapestry of human life. We are all interconnected. You have a vital part to play. Remember as well that you are being watched, especially by those who love you. You will not know how many people you will impact with your patient endurance until you face Jesus on your judgment day. Cling to Jesus, who is *the* answer, and let those around you learn what it is to endure through faith in Him. What a testimony you can be to Jesus's triumphant Spirit in you!

My dad had said in his earlier years that he would commit suicide if he were to become incapacitated in his senior years. In the beginning stages of his Alzheimer's disease, however, he surrendered his heart to Jesus, as you know. And Dad fought to live, right to the very end. In October 2018, I did not think Dad would make it until Christmas, but he died on April 29, 2019. He fought, and he fought, and he fought. With Jesus in you, you can too.

CHAPTER FORTY

SHAME

I encourage you to keep on because no matter what anyone says, there is shame associated with suicide. No matter what the circumstances, no matter what the situation, there is a black mark against the one who commits suicide, as well as against that person's family. No one ever commends the one who attempts suicide for his or her courage.

I felt engulfed in shame after I became disabled. It followed me everywhere and was nearly impossible to shake, especially first. It literally took years for me to feel loose from its grip.

Certainly, there is no pride for those who try to end their lives; there is no sense of victory. The victory and the pride can come after having successfully navigated through a period of deep suffering or after a failed suicide attempt, when the person grieves, picks up the pieces, and moves forward from there.

If you have attempted suicide in the past or feel you have done something terribly wrong and feel shame, go to Jesus. Ask for His forgiveness and receive it. There is healing for shame. Seek it, then brush yourself off. It takes strength from above to get up, stand, and begin walking again after a serious fall.

REMORSE AND REGRET

You cannot fully know what God is doing by allowing your suffering. His ways are mysterious (Isaiah 55:8–9). Should you rail against that and decide to make a suicide attempt as a Christian, you will experience deep remorse and regret, either this side of heaven, if you survive, or on the other side. Allow me to explain.

Because He has given us all free will, God can allow you to attempt suicide, but He can also allow you to be physically maimed somehow as a result of that attempt. I was banking on death and thought of nothing but Jesus at the time of my jump, but He had other plans. Thank the Lord I was spared quadriplegia, like Joni or a vegetative state, conditions that easily could have been the outcome. How many people have experienced kidney failure because of a drug overdose or have done serious damage to some other part of their bodies as a result of a suicide attempt?

Certainly, any suicide attempt carries with it profound emotional and spiritual scarring, for you and for those around you. The attempt not only weakens your faith but robs you of confidence and that feeling of victory you might have experienced, had you overcome the temptations that Satan hurled at you. Friends and loved ones may seriously question your ability to handle life; as a result, they may seek to overprotect and coddle.

A suicide attempt leaves a trail of folks who grieve and who often feel guilty, to one degree or another. All will be influenced—at least, disheartened; at most, suicidal themselves—by the seed of Satan that any attempted suicide leaves behind. Individuals may look back and feel regret and remorse when they take stock of what their attempt did to them and to others. Now, when you think of moving forward in your present situation, things may not seem so impossible if you think about what it takes to fall and then try to get back in the race.

Remember that if you die from the attempt, as a born-again believer, you will feel regret on the other side as well. You will go to heaven, yes, but Jesus will reveal to you what you would have experienced in later years and the contributions you would have made, had you persevered, as well as what He was trying to work in your precious character through the suffering. All suffering lasts only for a season. It will come to an end—somehow, someday.

You will eventually pass from this earth anyway. Instead of speeding up the process, why not hold off and wait to see what God has in store for you in the future? As it was with Job, it could be so much better than you have ever experienced!

HOW WILL YOU SPEND ETERNITY?

Christians who choose to end their lives must contend with a diminished eternity as a result. Remember—there is a direct correlation between how much you reached to the Lord while you were on the earth, including in your most desperate moments, and the quality of your eternity, including the depth and quantity of the "treasures in heaven" (Matthew 6:19–21), which will be your reward.

Did you let Satan waste your suffering, or did you surrender it to God to be used for His glory? Did you complain and sit in self-pity, taking little to no action, or did you reach for, seek, ask, and knock on the door of God's heart in your suffering?

I once said to a friend that when we reach our individual judgment days, we will have wished we had suffered more. It is through surrendering our suffering that we develop something that nothing else can accomplish—Christlike character. I crave that and am willing to endure whatever it takes for God to mold this in me. Can you make that commitment as well?

THE VULNERABLE

Those who are particularly vulnerable in society come in many forms; for example, the young, the elderly, those struggling with addictions, or the disabled (whether it be physical, psychiatric, or developmental). These folks may bring out in us our own vulnerability. They can get us in touch with our own deep pain, which can lead, for some, to discomfort and a feeling of being ill at ease. Often, such people have not come to terms with the weakness within themselves.

My mom had three cats. The one that recently, and unfortunately, had to be put down was very open to me and not the least bit afraid of the wheelchair, even though I almost backed into him on one occasion. The other two are deathly afraid of my chair and stay far from me, in general. So it is with people. Certain people warm up to me right away and can interact with me in a holistic and freeing way, treating me as they treat any other person; other folks shy away when they see me, avoiding me, and seeming ill at ease with me in my chair. While it's understandable that folks feel awkward, especially initially, around someone who looks different, hanging out with a disabled person, one can learn to relax in his or her presence. Perhaps then, they could more readily come to grips with that vulnerable part inside themselves that's triggered at the sight of a wheelchair.

I encourage you to get in touch with the child inside you who is that vulnerable and sensitive part of you. One good way to do this, aside from spending time with the physically handicapped, is to engage in godly counseling. Talking about how your little child feels or interacts with the adult you can be so healing. In doing so, you will be less likely to be put off by someone who approaches you in a vulnerable state.

Recall that Jesus was broken and spilled out, as the song says. He made Himself so vulnerable in order that you might enjoy eternal communion, not separation from the one who is love. Vulnerability, at its essence, has Jesus in it, for He embodied vulnerability at its core. He willingly embraced weakness, coming to earth earth as a helpless baby, for the Father's ultimate purpose and glory. If you are feeling vulnerable at this time, can you let God use it for His ultimate purpose and glory?

Paul embraced vulnerability as well:

I will boast all the more gladly about my weaknesses, so that Christ's power may rest on me. That is why, for Christ's sake, I delight in weaknesses. (2 Corinthians 12:9b–10a)

Incredibly, weakness is something about which Paul actually boasted. Can we follow his example and express healthy pride in that which makes us vulnerable?

In addition, Paul means for us, as Christians, to be all one body, all on equal ground (1 Corinthians 12:22–26). Someone once told me that at the foot of the cross, the ground is level. Everyone from any profession are all on par with each other in God's economy.

CHAPTER FORTY-ONE
FULL EQUALITY

Though we essentially are all equal, people are not treated as such in this world. There is prejudice against ethnicity and skin color, as examples. Those with physical disabilities also can have a real challenge, socially. People may feel heavy just by seeing them, and this can be a deterrent from regular or even light social interaction. Wheelchair athlete and author Rick Hansen has said, "My disability is that I cannot use my legs; my handicap is your negative perception of that disability and, thus, of me."

When an able-bodied friend and I come into a restaurant, for instance, the host/hostess immediately will interact with the able-bodied person. The able-bodied are somehow "easy" to interact with; they are seen as normal, whereas a disabled person is somehow seen as abnormal. It's understandable though, because the able-bodied far outnumber the physically disabled in the general population. Fact is, though, the disabled are just like everyone else—they laugh, cry, and dream like everyone else, although they may have the added stress of not having proper use of certain parts of their bodies.

It's a wonderful thing to learn the best way to help those who are different in some way, whether in wheelchairs or not. A friendly gesture, in the form of entering in, for instance, can go a long way. Those who are different may find themselves particularly connection-hungry. They may value so much when a person freely engages with them and overcomes that initial awkwardness.

Awkwardness also may be prevalent when others interact with someone with a known psychiatric disability. Stigma is real; whenever there is talk of "losing one's mind," people tend to get frightened, and a barrier of fear goes up. Those with psychiatric conditions are just like you, except they may have chemical malfunctioning in their brains.

The one who feels awkward around a person who has a psychiatric condition or who is in a wheelchair can, hopefully, come to see that though body shapes, sizes, or functionality (including mobility devices) may differ, we are all the same in terms of basic needs, hopes, dreams, and desires.

Though we are alike in many ways, if you have a psychiatric disability, are in a wheelchair, or have other characteristics that are not the norm, remember that your outstanding feature just makes you more outstanding, more unique, and more special in a good way. Remember Paul's words—that your weakness makes you "indispensable" (1 Corinthians 12:22). If you experience rejection because of this feature, know that God loves and embraces you just as you are. We all need the Creator to shower His love on us, His creation, in ways that fit our uniqueness.

THE FAMILY

Sometimes it's difficult to find the love we need within our own families. The dysfunctional family is a smaller unit of a society of fallen people. If that family is without Christ, how broken it can be. Especially in a crisis, even that family, though, can learn to pull together to help one another. That's what I witnessed when I became disabled. My mother and sister, both non-Christians, worked with me to help me create a home for myself. My sister, in particular, bought all the things necessary for my new life in an apartment setting. In fact, no one on the planet has helped me more, in a practical way, than my sister. Without her and my mom's help, I likely would still be living in that institution.

If your family members are not on board with seeking the love of God, that should not stop you from doing so. As you show them love and appreciation through the Holy Spirit, they can grow through you and your example. I watched as both my father and mother observed me and what I experienced, to the point that they exhibited a deep respect for me. My father even followed my lead into a relationship with Jesus, as you know. Through prayer and as you seek God as, perhaps, the sole Christian in your family, He will prune you and produce fruit of which all can partake. Within families, there is a special bond of love between the members, no matter how dysfunctional they may be. Capitalize and concentrate on this, if this describes you. Keep your focus on the love that is there, rather than on the dysfunction.

Sometimes, though, families can remain fragmented and broken, despite your best efforts. This can lead to profound disappointment and pain. Forgiveness is paramount, in this case, to release your family from blame. Dr. Charles Stanley suggests you dig into the Word to overcome discouragement and to keep doing this to stay free of discouragement's grip. You may also decide that you need some extra support, such as from a trained counselor, with whom you can dialogue on these issues.

I know it's very tough to love people who don't love you back or who are unkind, but remember the golden rule: "Do to others as you would have them do to you" (Luke 6:31). This rule still stands, regardless of the circumstances. Develop healthy boundaries, even with abusive relatives, and cling to Christ for strength, remaining faithful to the golden rule and hence, to God. If you fail to keep the golden rule, whether in your family or otherwise, know that God is a forgiving God, waiting with open arms to receive your repentance and embrace you, fully aware of your weaknesses and frailties as a human being.

Clearly, the family plays a crucial role in the health of its members. However, I cannot overstate the power and influence of a single healthy member in an otherwise dysfunctional family. Even estranged members are folks for whom you can pray. Remember, prayer changes things. Fear not if you are the only healthy one in your family. Rest assured that they are watching you and observing. Your example goes a long way. Look at where the example of Jesus has gone—all around the world to give joy and peace and eternal bliss to any and all who call on His name!

CHAPTER FORTY-TWO
ON THE LOVE OF CHRIST

*T*he love of Jesus is beyond description and beyond our comprehension.

> And I pray that you, being rooted and established in love, may have power, together with all the Lord's holy people, to grasp how wide and long and high and deep is the love of Christ, and to know this love that surpasses knowledge—that you may be filled to the measure of all the fullness of God. (Ephesians 3:17–19)

Jesus experiences love not only on a human level but, given his 100 percent divinity, on an eternal level. Indeed, the love that comes from God the Trinity is supernatural in nature. We cannot fathom the way God wants to love (Isaiah 55:8–9); that's where faith comes in. He asks us to trust His incomprehensible brand of love.

I would suggest that God has not only an eternal kind of love for us but also experiences eternal sadness. When we hurt ourselves in small ways, by belittling and demeaning ourselves, giving fuel to the devil's lies about us, or on a larger scale, with cutting or with the ultimate, suicide, God grieves in a way that is unique to Him.

> And do not grieve the Holy Spirit of God, with whom you were sealed for the day of redemption. (Ephesians 4:30)

Do you want to please God or sadden Him? Just as parents can be hurt by seeing the pain in their children's lives, by virtue of their relationship, Jesus can experience hurt as well as love toward us in a similar way. He was, after all, also 100 percent human, and we are called His children (Galatians 3:26; Hebrews 12:7, as examples).

Remember that the greatest commandment in scripture is to love the Lord your God with all that is in you, and the second greatest commandment is, "Love your neighbor as yourself" (Matthew 22:38). Loving God involves listening to and obeying His voice as He leads you to love Him, others, and yourself. He sees you in such a way that, in doing so, He models the way that you are to view yourself, concentrating on your potential, not on your faults. If you could look to Him and embrace your identity in Christ—who you are in Him as His child, as laid out in His Word—and not look to others, comparing yourself and diverting your gaze from Him, you would be well on your way to finding that spiritual health for which you search.

"God is love" (1 John 4:16). Cling to Him and to His amazing words of love today, and watch as He works. No other book is as alive and living as the Bible to a born-again believer, and it is through the Bible that He loves us in ways that fit our individuality. How many times has it happened that what I read in scripture is exactly what I need to hear? Jesus can so tailor His Word to our specific situation that sometimes it leaves us astonished. And that's a main way He loves on us, which is why it's so important to have that quiet time daily with just you and the Bible.

ON THE BODY

I speak once again to those who have ever seriously contemplated suicide.

As a Christian, God lives in your body in the form of the Holy Spirit (1 Corinthians 6:19–20), as you well know. You were drawn to Him by this third person of the Trinity. It was God who revealed the truth to you so you could step into relationship with Christ. Your body is the storehouse, the home of God in you.

Did you make your kidneys? Can you do what your liver does for you? Do you keep your heart pumping? Do you keep yourself breathing at night? God is at work in you in ways that you likely do not often think about and may even take for granted. I encourage you to study the human body and expose yourself to the workings of the wonderful creation of God that you are. In doing so, it can help you develop a deep sense of awe and respect for the miracle that is you.

Scripture says, "I am fearfully and wonderfully made" (Psalm 139:14). Sometimes, we don't realize that we had good health until something goes wrong. My roommate in the institution once said to me, "You don't miss the water 'til the well runs dry." So true!

Sometimes things go wrong with our bodies out of sheer wear and tear, the process of aging, or perhaps from our own neglect. Satan is subtle, and he can veer us away from efforts to care well for ourselves. The evil one craves destruction, whereas Jesus is the Author, Creator, and Sustainer of life on earth and in the hereafter:

> All things have been created through Him and for Him. He is before all things, and in Him all things hold together. (Colossians 1:16b–17)

We make choices every day regarding with whom we want to side.

Although our bodies wear down because of the introduction of sin in the garden of Eden (again, the devil's work), recognize that these bodies of ours are on loan. Tending healthily to our physical needs and filling our minds and hearts with good, healthy, godly things is crucial.

CHAPTER FORTY-THREE
OTHER PROPHETS

*S*cripture speaks of others who experienced attacks from the enemy and fell into despair. Prophets such as Moses (Numbers 11:15), Jonah (Jonah 4:3), and Elijah (1 Kings 19:4) all had been suicidal. In Elijah's case, God instructed him to eat and drink. Elijah obeyed God and took some food to revive himself; he also had some rest (1 Kings 19:8). Taking good care of the body cannot be overemphasized; this discipline is so very important, not only for our physical well-being but also for managing our emotions. Our emotions are intricately connected to our bodily functions.

When I went for an interview for a to-die-for internship position, I made sure to go to the washroom prior to the interview (I was not in the wheelchair at that time). Sometime into the interview, I suddenly had the urge to go again. I quickly but politely excused myself and made a beeline for the washroom. Because of my performance anxiety, I did not make it—and I was mortified! Thankfully, I was wearing very dark-colored pants that did not show the stain as much.

I regained my composure, reentered the interview room, placed my coat on the chair, sat down, and continued with the interview. When it came time to leave, I wanted to make another beeline—for the elevator, this time—but the interviewer insisted on going with me. I was doubly mortified. What if she smelled something? What if she noticed? As the elevator doors swung open, I saw that the walls in the elevator were made of mirrors! Triply mortified!

Sometime later, I told the interviewer what had happened. She said she'd never noticed a thing—or perhaps she was too kind to tell me otherwise. Has your body ever functioned in unusual ways when you were under unusual stress? (By the way, I got the position for which I was interviewed.)

In caring well for our bodies, exercise gives us energy; dissipates the power of difficult emotions, like rage and anger; and provides for the physical muscles what trials do for our faith muscles. Exercise can be as simple as going for a daily walk. Prior to my injury, I walked seven days a week for thirty minutes each time. Even now, I own an exercise machine for people with disabilities called a MOTOmed. It pedals my legs for me and has an arm bike attachment. I use this machine virtually every day. I have exercised throughout my life. Mom enrolled my siblings and me in swimming lessons from the time we were young. As a teenager, I did competitive synchronized swimming. I realized, in hindsight, that those vigorous weekly workouts helped me deal with the rage deep inside of me as a result of the abuse I experienced as a child. They gave me an outlet for that intense emotion.

Speaking of developing our faith muscles, God said of Job, "There is no one on earth like him; he is blameless and upright, a man who fears God and shuns evil" (Job 1:8). Clearly, Job was already super-special in God's eyes, and God was ready and willing to allow Job to be tested.

When this happened, Job fell into the depths of despair. He cursed the day he was born rather extensively and wished for death (e.g., Job 3:3, 11, 16).

Despite these very heavy feelings, he persevered. In fact, he spent many chapters expressing his emotions, getting his anguish out to try to make sense of what had happened. He did all this, despite the inadequacies of his "comforters." Job's faith muscle simply grew stronger and stronger through his reeling and venting. In fact, it was by way of his reeling and venting that his faith enlarged and was able to sustain him.

If you are in a particularly dark place, maybe you need to do some talking—maybe a lot of talking—and some venting and reeling as well. Get those dark feelings out; they need to come out. Aside from sitting with Job in silence for the first week after his trials, the very best thing Job's friends did for him was to let him talk. His friends listened poorly, but they did give Job airtime to speak as much as he needed.

Job confronted his friends but also God. If you feel bold enough to do this, remember Job. The Lord's response to Job's query of Him was, "Brace yourself like a man; I will question you and you shall answer me" (Job 38:3; 40:7). Be prepared for a tough answer, if one comes at all, for God is not compelled to explain Himself or give His reasons for doing what He does.

In His response to Job, the Lord elaborated on His greatness:

> "Where were you when I laid the earth's foundations? Tell me, if you understand. Who marked off its dimensions? Surely you know!" (Job 38:4–5a)

Job recognized that he had had some pride and had not considered the inconceivable vastness of God and His power when he spoke to God. His response to God, in turn, was abject repentance (Job 42:6). We too need to be reminded of God's majesty and of His eternal nature when we face something that seems unbearable.

Try not to get stuck in the feelings of the moment. Moses, Jonah, Elijah, and Job all got past their deep dark feelings. They were all mighty men of God, proving that no one is immune to deep despair or even suicidal thoughts, including those who are very close to and favored by God.

CHAPTER FORTY-FOUR

COMFORTING PRESENCE

*M*aybe you are at the end of your rope and find those around you to be far from a comfort, as Job did. When you suffer tremendously, remember that you are not alone. There are people who need regular dialysis in order to live and find it nearly impossible to travel. Others need wheelchairs; some need stretchers; some live in constant or near-constant pain; some have family members with addictions; some have addictions; some have had surgery that was botched; some have to wait and wait for the surgery they desperately need; some are homeless and young; some are housebound and elderly; some live in institutions; some have been through natural disasters; some have lived through horrific car wrecks—you get the idea. We all have our crosses to bear. The rest of the human race has also had its fair share of trouble.

You are not alone. You may *feel* alone; you are not. Of course, we also have God living inside us as born-again believers. He's that close. Let the presence of others who suffer right along with you and the presence of God be your comfort. The support and strength for which we yearn ultimately comes entirely from God, although He works through others—His creation. During COVID-19, despite the hardship this has brought, I have seen people coming together to help one another, sometimes in extraordinary ways. One woman, for instance, was highlighted on the news for sewing masks for frontline workers. Some celebrities have put on benefit concerts to help raise money for the cause. Mail deliverers created a convoy of their trucks and made a trek around hospitals, honking in support of the nurses, doctors, and other hospital staff who are risking their lives each day to help others. There has been a genuine sense that we are all in this together.

Certainly, we can learn from others who have persevered through deep trials. I love to read and hear about testimonies of folks who have been through tremendous trials and come out the other end. Others can glean comfort as they see people struggle and come victoriously through hard times. Courage begets courage. Perhaps that is one of the reasons that Jesus promises that we will have trouble (see John 16:33), so we can witness and be inspired by one another's courage.

Those who have been raised in a form of isolation, emotionally and/or spiritually, who were somehow ostracized or rejected by the family, and/or who are living disconnected from their loved ones can feel most alone and vulnerable in their troubles, as if they are the only ones going through such deep waters. They can hold on to the lie that what they are experience is unique (it is, in a way, as we are all on an individual journey, but it isn't, in another way, because there are others in the world who have felt the same way). They might feel they are deeply inferior to others; contrarily, they may hold the belief that they are above everyone else, believing they have courage and wisdom that others do not. Though they may even live in a family of others who suffer alongside of them, they do not feel a sense of community. Instead, they feel thrust into their own little boxes. This is what I experienced, being the family scapegoat. I felt disconnected from them—as if I somehow had green skin and that I was ugly and stupid.

When a person feels disconnected from others, even from God, that person can get used to feeling like that and can register it as normal. This type of sufferer can glean much from a consistent, trained person, learning what it is to reach out and eventually find strength in community. A Christian counselor can provide a sense of God's comforting presence "in the flesh," so that a sufferer can eventually learn to embrace and rest in God's presence on his or her own. As another human being who has suffered, such a therapist can provide a deeper form of healthy human connection, both emotionally and spiritually, that was perhaps absent in the early years of the client. As a reminder, reaching out to safe people whom we can trust and to God in times of pain is certainly what Jesus modeled in His garden of Gethsemane.

Resting in His presence is enriching and refreshing. He can enfold you in a warm blanket of love and support, as you learn to let Him deeply in.

A DYNAMIC RELATIONSHIP

Our relationship with Jesus can be dynamic, which is defined as energetic, active, and potent. It certainly is alive in the life of the born-again believer. Jesus hurts when we do. He rejoices when we do. He mourns when we do, as He calls us to do with each other (Romans 12:15). He actively comes alongside us when we hurt, reaching down, drawing near, and reminding us that He has been there too.

After his series of calamities, when he was likely tempted to give up, instead, Job said, "The Lord gave and the Lord has taken away" (Job 1:21b). What strength Job showed in saying this! Certainly Job's relationship with God was deeply dynamic. I pray that you seek and are given the strength to cling to Him in the very midst of *your* turmoil and that you can hear His voice say to you, as He said to their storm when the disciples were afraid for their lives (Mark 4:35–41), "Quiet! Be still!"

If your storm involves thoughts of suicide, know that suicide is a turning away, a lack of trust, a closing the door in life's face—indeed, in Christ's face—since "all things have been created by him and for him" (Colossians 1:16b). It's exclaiming, "He can't!" or more accurately, perhaps, "I won't let Him!" He created you for His purposes, mysterious though they may be (Isaiah 55:8–9). Won't you allow Him to work those purposes in your life?

Attempting suicide is saying that Jesus doesn't know what He is doing in allowing your suffering. Though your pain may be unspeakable and relentless, I encourage you not to give up. Draw from the strength of Job, and let God, in His energetic, active, and potent way, work in you through your trial.

CHAPTER FORTY-FIVE
ON FREE WILL

As a reminder: God allows suicide because He has given us free will. Suicide, however, may be seen as an acceptable way of coping when individuals have reached their limit—when they can bear no more and can't go on for one more day. Or could they? For years, I believed that if things got really hard, I could always take my life. It took my being physically maimed for me to think differently. A prayer of Moses in Psalm 90:12 is one that I have put to memory: "Teach us to number our days aright, that we may gain a heart of wisdom." I pray this for you as well.

A friend once said, "Yesterday is dead and buried, and tomorrow is too far away." Gazing too far ahead or too far behind can be real dangers. To look into the past to find resolution for hurt feelings, as one would do in healthy counseling, is one thing, but to be fixated on it is another.

Paul says, "Forgetting what is behind and straining toward what is ahead, I press on toward the goal to win the prize for which God has called me heavenward in Christ Jesus" (Philippians 3:13b–14). Paul is giving instruction on how to choose to move forward in this difficult life—we are to be heaven-minded.

Make the choice to live in the present, pressing on to the future. Let God comfort you where you are today. Use your free will to soak in the Word, to commune with Jesus in prayer, and to talk with Him and to helpful others, all the while listening for that still, small voice—the one He uses to strengthen, guide, and love you. He's waiting with open arms to receive you in *this* way.

SERVICE

Faith is the bridge between the temporal and the eternal; it is the muscle that lies between these two joints. Suffering can strengthen the faith muscle to the point that we become more aware of Jesus's suffering in others. And it is this widened faith that can spur us on to good deeds and to service to "the least of these" (Matthew 25:40) that we see around us. There is no other high that surpasses that which one feels when one is in active service for the Lord.

"As the body without the spirit is dead, so faith without deeds is dead" (James 2:26). As Christians, we can ask the Lord to place us into service for Him. Even those who are housebound or bedridden can pray; as the saying goes, "Prayer changes things." Those who cannot work at a paid position can do volunteer work and be used for God's glory. Don't underestimate the help you can give by reading the Word to a lonely senior in a nursing home or to a disabled person in a long-term care facility. Needs can be so great in such places, however. We may find ourselves saying to ourselves, "But I'm only one person! I can only do so much!" One giving person can accomplish a lot of good; don't you doubt it! Think of the cumulative effect of many persons working together. What an army for good we can be!

ASSUMING

It strikes me that it is especially important for individuals contemplating suicide to have a clear sense of where they will go after they leave this earth. Assuming that God will honor them as good people, who lived good lives and therefore should go to heaven, has sealed an eternal destiny of doom for many, I'm sure. Satan is called "the prince of this world" (John 12:31). He offers such promises, as well as the pleasures of this world—physical luxury, comfort, and ease. I notice that those who have been left alone by him and have the goodies of this world lavished on them may be in a very perilous situation indeed. There were psalmists who wondered why the wicked prosper and the righteous suffer (e.g.,

Psalm 73:3; 94:3). Success in the world may be offered to those who have this world and worldly gain in mind—expensive cars, lavish homes, big bank accounts. Dr. Charles Stanley says that if your heart is bent on accumulating stuff like this, in the end, it amounts to ashes, if you fail to receive the Lord's forgiveness for your sins.

Whatever is built for the kingdom is what truly lasts. How many have been satisfied with earthly pleasures, unaware of the spiritual riches available to them through Jesus Christ? Granted, there are some very wealthy Christians, but many, if not all, put their money to good use for the service of God.

The devil also suggests that your good works will outweigh your bad ones and that this will get you to heaven when you die. He promises a works-oriented salvation, as other religions offer, where being a good person and doing good deeds will gain you entrance into heaven. How do you know when you have done enough? How exhausting! Contrarily, Jesus offers His salvation by grace as *a gift* (Ephesians 2:8–9), as well as His rest to any and all who come to Him (Matthew11:28–30). How many very pious and genuinely religious people die, assuming that their good works will get them into heaven, only to face eternal, horrific destruction when it comes to their judgment day?

Truth can be difficult. Certainly, life is difficult. Seeking a relationship with Jesus by receiving His forgiveness for our sins is the *only* way to get to heaven when we die. Period.

CHAPTER FORTY-SIX

THERE CAN COME A POINT

Suicide is a decision you cannot take back. There can come a point when we decide to carry out our plans, where we're through with talking, where a decision has been made. I suggest to you that such a decision is made on inadequate and inaccurate information. Allow me to explain.

You may be at a point where you are still listening, still seeking input, and are still in the process of making your decision. Please mark this: if only you could see yourself and your situation through God's eyes; if only you could see His purposes and reasons for allowing what you are going through; if only you could feel His compassion and His tender love for you at this time, in and through your pain, you might find some peace and contentment, rather than the tossing and turmoil in which you may find yourself, teetering on a life-or-death decision. I pray that the gentle love and perspective of Jesus will reach you before you come to a point when you're through listening.

COLLABORATIVE EFFORT—THE DEFINITION OF SELF

When individuals ponder suicide, they may think that they are the only ones involved in the decision to end their lives. By the word *self*, one might think of a single entity, perhaps in three parts: body, soul, and spirit. But I contend that self is made up of a collaborative effort of all the people who have helped us, not to mention our Creator.

> For you created my inmost being; you knit me together in my mother's womb. (Psalm 139:13)

God made us and is ultimately in charge of all that we are in every way. Indeed, He can allow anything to go wrong at any time; there is someone bigger in control.

You are also a compilation of the love and attention your parents and siblings and friends gave you, as well as your teachers and influential secondary folk. Sometimes we can have a meeting that changes our lives. Something someone says sticks in our minds, or a loving gesture or thoughtful act touches our hearts. Perhaps someone supported you in prayer, if not in other ways. We carry with us part of the heart of each person who cared or cares about us, and those people's hearts will not ever be the same if *self* chooses harm in the ultimate way—with premature death.

We are not an island. I'll say it again: we are interconnected, all of us. People are waiting and watching. Take your role in the web seriously. We need each other's strength and courage interdependently.

A BLESSING, NOT A BURDEN

When I was going through deep, dark waters, I said to a friend that I did not want to be a burden to him. He responded, "You're not a burden. You're a blessing!" At the time, that comment caused me to stop and do a double-take. I had been at home, feeling as though I was a burden as that's how I felt as a child and in vulnerable situations like the one I was in at the time, so hearing his words was revolutionary for me.

Have you ever felt as though you were a burden? For those who feel like this, words such as my friend spoke can be so liberating. What a different perspective my friend had than the negative one I held.

What about vulnerable people in your life? What message are you sending to them? Are you revealing through your words and actions that they are a blessing or a burden? What can you do to help such people to feel like they are a blessing? What are you feeling if you are that vulnerable one?

Know that regardless of how you feel because of the actions or words of others, you *are* a blessing to God. You are His creation that He called "very good" (Genesis 1:31). Don't allow the enemy to lie to you that you are not infinitely precious and a blessing in God's sight. Joyce Meyer says that we are all God's favorites.

And you, strong one, share the wealth. Give from your heart and from the spiritual riches that come to you from Christ to help those more vulnerable feel special and blessed. As you give your heart to others in His service, God can give you spiritual riches from deep in *His* heart.

ON LIES

Once again, thoughts of suicide flash across the mind of virtually every adult living in this messy, difficult world at some point or another. It is also true that when one attempts suicide, one faces death. Although suicide does take courage, it reveals a dedication to *a series of lies*—that things cannot improve, that you are not going to feel different about your suffering in time, and that suffering does not serve an eternal purpose.

Jesus is trying to mold us more into His likeness in *His* way. It is through suffering, in particular, that He wishes us to reach to Him in humility and repentance. Pride can hinder growth; we may be stuck in independence or denial. Or we might suffer innumerable trials and remain bitter and hard-hearted, closed off to help, including that of a divine nature. Some from my family of origin, sadly, have chosen this road.

Endurance itself has a way of bringing new insight and perspective. It begs us to dig, to do emotional and spiritual work to understand. It calls us to look up; it can cause us to contemplate what death will hold, as well. We may try to grasp eternal things. Suffering is the spur God uses to cause us to gallop to Him, seeking answers. Sometimes answers don't come. Again, I remind you of Isaiah 55:8-9. Though we may not understand His ways, Christ will give you the strength to face your truth.

> The Lord is faithful, and he will strengthen and protect you from
> the evil one. (2 Thessalonians 3:3)

When I cursed God when I went to live in the institution, I was hanging on to a series of lies that caused me to see no way out of there. I saw no future for myself. I believed I would live and die in that place. But true to Romans 8:28, slowly, He changed my heart, and forgave. He has not yet healed my paralysis, but He renovated my heart back to Him. Let Him do the same for you, if you have found yourself veering off course because of intense suffering.

CHAPTER FORTY-SEVEN

BLACK-AND-WHITE THINKING

Black-and-white thinking can encourage us toward heavy hearts—indeed, toward suicide. With this tendency, one idealizes people as being much better than they actually are or idealizes in reverse, fantasizing them as being terrible ogres. It's a tendency to see the world in extremes. This can stem from childhood or adult trauma. Black-and-white thinking can make it difficult for such a one to make and sustain friendships, as he or she would be prone to develop extreme views of people he or she only just met. The isolation this can produce can lead to suicidal ideation.

If you think you may be living with black-and-white thinking, it can be very painful. Such sufferers can come to expect perfection, not only from themselves, but from others as well. It can be an all-or-nothing way of thinking. The people with whom those individuals interact either have it all and are fantastic, or they are judged negatively without even being given a chance. These attitudes can carry over onto God as well.

It is only as such a one consistently and persistently reaches to God over time that that one can come to know Him for who He is. However, we, as humans in general, gravitate toward each other. Author Sarah Young has said that when we are with others, we tend to forget about God and concentrate on pleasing those we are with. Again, we need to hide ourselves away to have a specific and intimate daily prayer time with God. Though it's a challenge, prayer can be a dialogue of a deeply healing nature. As you reach to Him, you can learn to rest in His presence. All of us need to do this, but it is especially crucial if you have black-and-white thinking. It can lead you into a healthy therapeutic relationship or healing program. There, you may get and stay connected to a safe person or people, something you may presently lack or that which may have been lacking in your childhood. As you get to know your therapist or your group leader, you can learn to rest in the safety and warmth of acceptance, thereby finding healing and relief. Slowly, as dialogue about it is shared, the extremes in thinking and the idealization can lift and heal. The jagged edges can be smoothed over.

Know that there is healing for the extremes of black-and-white thinking, and, with help, those individuals can find themselves making room for gray areas and being more flexible in their views.

TRYING TOO HARD

Trying too hard can spiral into suicidal ideation. Allow me to explain.

A little girl, for instance, lacked a consistent, healthy connection and dependence on her parents from a young age. In addition, she did not have the regular affirmation and encouragement every child needs and deserves. As she grows, she finds herself being prone to insecurity and feels the need to work herself toward acceptance by others.

Such a child is doubly in fear of rejection. Because she did not feel accepted early on, it takes only a hint of what she perceives as rejection from another to trigger this core reservoir of hurt. She ends up putting much stock in what she believes others feel about her, as she lacked that foundation of acceptance. Sometimes, she almost expects (and often unconsciously seeks) rejection because it is what is familiar to her. She craves acceptance but feels at home with rejection; it's what she deserves, she feels, because that's what she felt from her primary caregivers. They, after all, must be right. She hangs on to those feelings, which hamper her growth. She believes she is not worthy of true love, so if and when it comes, she does not know how to receive it. It feels so foreign to her, like a pauper wearing silk. Her efforts to relate have to transcend this core of hurt, and so, in the eyes of others, she tries too hard. It's a vicious circle because this trying too hard—trying to make up for inadequacies and earlier rejections—tends to put people off and can lead to actual rejection in itself. If this tendency persists into adulthood, it can lead to her finding herself suicidal.

If you think you are a person who tries too hard, rest assured that Jesus accepts and embraces you fully. He knows all about you—including all your weaknesses and flaws—and loves you just as you are. There is great healing found in receiving the love of Jesus.

In my bedroom, I have a picture of Jesus cradling a wounded lamb. He is holding that lamb so close to His breast that part of His face is concealed. When I look at it, I think of how He seeks to comfort me every minute. Indeed, I am never alone and never unloved, though I may not always feel it. If you find yourself trying too hard, try to realize that Jesus holds you ever so close to Him, if you are willing to accept His gentle embrace. He causes the little girl or little boy inside the adult to rest and cease striving. He lifts their heaviness.

There is deep healing for this tendency of trying too hard in a healthy therapeutic environment or similar program. In time, the acceptance and gentleness of a godly therapist or group leader can help smooth over and calm the need in the client to strive to such an extreme extent.

KEEP YOUR ETERNITY IN MIND

Our souls are not temporary but eternal. In light of this, I encourage you to keep your eternity in mind.

Eternity is unfathomable. So it is that we are sometimes called to unfathomable suffering—suffering beyond our scope to understand. God does this because

He is forging our eternity for us. In doing this, Jesus acts or allows something that we might feel is unreasonable. He is, by His nature, unreasonable (by finite, human standards).

Paul says,

> Join with me in suffering for the gospel, by the power of God. He has saved us and called us to a holy life—not because of anything we have done but because of his own purpose and grace. (2 Timothy 1:8–9)

It strikes me that part of God's purpose in allowing extreme suffering is because He had to make eternal restitution. He had to make eternal compensation for Adam and Eve's decision in the garden of Eden. He had to annihilate sin on an eternal level—that's why He allows so much suffering in the lives of Christians. Since our souls are eternal—the very same quality as God—it is through suffering alongside Jesus and clinging to Him that we, as born-again believers, become more like Him, gaining qualities we can enjoy, such as the fruits of the Spirit: love, joy, peace, longsuffering or forbearance or patience, kindness, goodness, faithfulness, gentleness, and self-control, both now and into the hereafter.

God knows and sees your eternity. Believe that God will use suffering in your life or in the life of a close friend or loved one to bring you closer to Him and to forge for you a deeper eternity. He knows it sometimes takes drastic steps to bring you to Him, and He will stop at nothing to do just that. He knows there is nothing better than for you to commune closely with Him. He knows that you would want that too, even if it takes intense suffering to produce that.

Jesus entrusts certain suffering to you because He hopes you will use it as a catalyst to promote growth in your faith and in your intimacy with Him. I'll say it again—there is a direct correlation between the time we spend with Him here on earth and the quality of our eternity. Seek Him now; you will thank Him later. He cares for you so much that He's willing to go to extreme measures to get your attention—to cause you to sit up and take notice of His infinite and sovereign power in your life. He knows His character in you will last forever.

God knows all. He ultimately is more concerned for your eternity and for your character than for your comfort. Try to keep that in mind.

CHAPTER FORTY-EIGHT
INTRUSIVENESS

*J*esus is a gentleman. His love is nonintrusive. He does not force us to say or do anything. He merely waits until we are ready to come to Him. Waiting is what He is, since He is love, and "love is patient," first of all (1 Corinthians 13:4).

It is possible to try to force trust. This can happen particularly with those starving for connection or with those who feel desperate to help someone they deem as needy; this is especially true for those who themselves were parentified, for example. Such folk can find themselves running ahead of the natural trust that gradually develops between two people who spend time together, demanding deep connection right away.

Trust—so very fragile and precious—must be married with patience, if any relationship or friendship is to last and be mutually beneficial. For one who is intrusive, counseling (or the like) can teach him or her that trust blossoms over time in any relationship, including a therapeutic one. From that, this individual can learn to take the gentlemanly stance of our Savior—to watch and wait as trust is slowly built. He or she can then learn to accept and be content with that slower, healthier pace.

In relationships and friendships, those in a hurry can seem to "pounce on" people. Those who do this need to follow Jesus's example and behave respectfully with regard to the boundaries of others. If you can relate to this, be gentle with yourself. Remember that learning appropriate boundaries can sometimes take a lifetime. Sometimes, it takes good help too, whether from a patient friend, relative, counseling professional, or group leader.

UNCOMFORTABLE TRUTH

In my relationship with Jesus, I sometimes am frustrated because His eternal nature eludes me. I want to know all the answers right *now.* Can you relate? We may seek to understand Him but find ourselves only getting angry at the way Jesus reveals the truth or at the truth itself, with which He confronts us. This can be the case especially when in therapy. Sometimes I know I've had a good session when I become angry and reticent with the therapist for leading me into an uncomfortable truth.

You might feel this way at God or at a truth-telling friend, loved one, or professional in your life. Perhaps you have someone in your life who tells you the truth, rather than what you want to hear. Truth is, life is difficult. Truth is, sometimes hearing it can cause us to boil inside because coming to grips with it can be so very challenging.

Jesus, grant us strength to receive Your truth for us and to embrace it, no matter how uncomfortable it may feel, as You say that it is the very thing that "will set ... [us] free" (John 8:32).

WORKAHOLICS/INTIMACY

Some have learned to bury themselves in work. Disregarding leisure, some hide from intimacy with others, leaning toward becoming workaholics. They may feel guilty if they are not producing. Perhaps they were raised in a family with a strong work ethic and/or an unwritten understanding that the children must do well in school, without receiving any praise or affirmation when they did. Excelling was just expected of them.

Perhaps they have not been exposed to extended bonding, "down" times within our families. This can add to a feeling of heaviness when they become adults. As a result, they may not be able to learn to feel that emotional intimacy within the family unit that is so crucial to developing healthily. Experiencing such bonding times can be strengthening, relaxing, and renewing.

We don't need to wait until we're presentable to approach Jesus. That's good news, especially to the workaholics, who often believe they have to work themselves into acceptance. Jesus accepts us just as we are, and by being in the very presence of victory personified, we can find that He emanates peace and comfort. We need simply to plop our weary bodies at His feet and soak Him in.

Our need, as humans, is for both the horizontal and the vertical, as is depicted in the shape of the cross. Don't let your push to do work keep you from reaching out to others and joining in on fellowship times and in small group meetings. Work is important—yes—but don't allow it to consume you.

Developing spiritual intimacy with God and interdependence with others—no matter who you are but especially for the workaholic—is essential in the healing of a heavy heart. And it helps keep you from developing suicidal thoughts.

MORE ON PRAYER

When trials get intense, realize that suicidal despair is a gift that speaks to the urgency of seeking God. Reaching out to your community can be so important purely because your own personal prayer time can be so very difficult when you are in despair. When we are despairing, we especially and desperately need the prayers of others. Job himself said,

> To him who is afflicted, kindness should be shown by his friend,
> even though he forsakes the fear of the Almighty. (Job 6:14)

We may, in fact, end up turning from God. Anger at the Savior is a major barrier to communion with our Creator. Know that He can take your anger. Job expressed anger at God when he asked Him why he was not stillborn (Job 3:16), for example. Go ahead and rail, if you must. Again, get those dark emotions out of you.

Job certainly forsook "the fear of the Almighty," as is evident from his response, after he finally spoke with God: "Surely I spoke of things I did not understand, things too wonderful for me to know. Therefore I despise myself and repent in dust and ashes" (Job 42:3, 6).

I remind you of Paul's writing to the Corinthian church, when he and Timothy had "despaired of life itself" (2 Corinthians 1:8). They relied on and leaned on God; they also openly entreated the Corinthians to pray for them (2 Corinthians 1:10a–11). The prayers of others are a vital support as we go through the process of suffering. If you find it hard to pray, ask God to help you to reach out to Him and to His people.

God knows we are not perfect, that there are many distractions, that Satan is alive and active in our lives, especially if we are strong believers. Despite all this, I encourage you to try to make the effort. Sit before an empty chair. Imagine the Great Physician resting in that chair. Or talk to a picture of Jesus that moves or stirs you, as I do. Pour your heart out to Him, trusting that He hears all and understands more than you know.

Go to him, as the song says, "Just as I am." His love is higher, deeper, and richer than the love we have received here on earth from others. As you go to Him, He'll embrace you and love you whole, as you share your pain with Him. "You do not have because you do not ask God" (James 4:2). Go to Him about anything and everything.

Many times, when things get very tough, it's sheer perseverance alone that gets us through—a sheer determination to hang in there. When our situation surrounds us, Satan can tempt us with such thoughts as, *What's it all for?* or *It'll never get better*, as well as the what-ifs, the if-onlys, and the tormenting whys. This is why, by an act of our will, we need to set our hearts and our minds on things above.

> Since … you have been raised with Christ, set your hearts on things above, where Christ is, seated at the right hand of God. (Colossians 3:1–2)

> Finally, brothers and sisters, whatever is true, whatever is noble, whatever is right, whatever is pure, whatever is lovely, whatever is admirable—if anything is excellent or praiseworthy—think about such things. (Philippians 4:8)

By an act of our will, we need to seek out God in things that can encourage, not drag us down: Christian books (His book), movies, music, and people who uplift. Again, it's so crucial to seek His wisdom regarding with whom and with what you spend your precious God-given time. Let Christ, His divine optimism and positive people buoy you up.

Jesus may speak to you countless times throughout a day. Learn to be sensitive to hear that still, small voice. Prayer is the key to a rich, spiritual life. It brings joy and releases feelings of helplessness and hopelessness. It is something you can do when all else is beyond you. Make prayer a regular part of your daily life. Truly, to be able to pray is to be free.

RESPONSIBILITIES

As long as we are on this earth, we will have responsibilities, sometimes very heavy ones. Certainly, we will always have the responsibility of caring well for ourselves as adults, something that sometimes can be arduous. If you are a parent, you have the added tremendous responsibility of also caring for your little people. Even children have responsibilities—perhaps with pets, doing their chores, helping out around the house. As we surrender our responsibilities to Jesus in prayer, He can offer His direction and strength.

Sometimes keeping up with responsibilities can be daunting and difficult indeed. You may have financial debts and find it difficult to keep up with all the expenses. Perhaps you have been left alone to go on without your partner, or perhaps you have struggled with what feels like an overwhelming load of care for as long as you can remember, even from your youth. Perhaps you, as a child, were asked to support your stressed-out parent(s) or were forced into a role of peacemaker when the family was in turmoil. Perhaps you are a caregiver to a relative with serious health problems. Maybe it's your nagging health problem or pain that tends to drag you down and hinders you from full enjoyment of your day. Such relentless responsibilities can contribute to or create a heavy heart, even promote suicidal thoughts.

You cannot control what happens to you, but you can control the way you handle your spirit and your emotions, which comprise the seat of your soul. It is your responsibility to learn how to communicate your feelings without being merely reactive or accusatory. Practice saying things like, "When you do or say _____, I feel _____," rather than "You make me feel _____."

Learn to take responsibility for your feelings. By that, I mean owning them. If children are not taught or modeled how to deal effectively with their emotions, their feelings can get bottled up inside them, or worse, they may become explosive. If this was you, it may be necessary to seek the safety and additional guidance of a counselor or appropriate program to learn to express yourself effectively. In therapy, you can practice and learn more social skills. Such a professional needs to be a person who creates an accepting environment in which you can "swim," whatever your feelings or attitudes. A good therapist can help you make serious and positive changes in your life; programs like Celebrate Recovery can do this as well.

Journaling feelings can be helpful. Journal entries may be used as fuel for a counseling session. Learning to articulate feelings takes practice. You can try it with trusted friends, as well as with your therapist. Where possible, using humor can lighten the way and rejuvenate. The Holy Spirit creates joy. When He is present in two people conversing, a lightness can carry the conversation and can create a time of playful repartee. I experience this with a few friends of mine.

While we need others horizontally, the only one God wants us to be dependent on is Him. God is the ultimate source of all the help we get from others anyway, so it makes sense to put our full dependence on Him. It's all part of taking good care of ourselves, a responsibility from which we will not be free this side of heaven.

<small>CHAPTER FORTY-NINE</small>

EVERY LITTLE BIT COUNTS

Exercise is so important, especially for those with heavy hearts. As a reminder, walks are especially helpful; they have a way of generating energy and endorphins as well as dispelling depression. Feelings of despair and suicidal ideation can be lightened as we discipline ourselves to exercise.

If you have had some sort of injury, are unable to do what you used to do, and are relegated to physiotherapy, do your exercises. Embrace your present reality and your current abilities. Work hard at your recovery, and if recovery does happen—fantastic. If not—with a spinal cord injury, perhaps, or multiple sclerosis—the only thing left to do is to embrace the truth of your specific individual situation, and do and use what you can.

When I lived in the institution, there was a physio room with a few exercise machines. Early on, I felt little effect and thought the physio was a waste of time. But as I persisted with it, little by little, I could see benefits; it gave me a feeling of lightness. Eventually, I looked forward to it. Now, I use my own exercise machine almost daily.

As you are faithful to putting energy into your well-being, God can take it and flood you with His strength and His blessings. Rest assured that He sees your every effort and is right there with you in it. Every little bit counts.

THE WAY WE DIE

The way we die is important.

If we die with victory and honor, there is a legacy of pride and relief for those left behind. They are left with what I call "positive mourning"—grief that does not last forever but is resolved in a shorter time. With the death of my father, I wailed on the day I heard of his passing, but other than that, I cried little, simply because I was so proud of him; I admired him for accepting Jesus into his heart in his senior years, and for his enduring to the very end. Admittedly, I did have a stay in hospital as my depression flared up, even despite this, a sense of closure came more quickly, a resting and a peace—for me, at least. I admired Dad so because he fought so hard to live, despite the fact that he was nearly bedridden near the end and that his quality of life was minimal. Days before he passed, he had said to his sitter, "I have to go." The sitter then asked him, "Where are you going, Ron?" He answered, "I don't know." With his Alzheimer's, he had forgotten that he was a Christian, bound for heaven!

Though we may not fully understand the reason for our suffering, we need to allow ourselves to come to a victorious death by resting in faith and reminding ourselves that Jesus has everything in His sovereign control. If you are reading this from palliative care, please realize that He knows what He is doing, both for our good as Christians and for the good of those around us, by allowing us to suffer as we do.

We are asked to work diligently in the midst of our grief, to seek Jesus and His will. If that despair is driving you to have thoughts of suicide, make the choice—though it may seem monumental—to take that first step with God to reach out. Remember, it is up to us, ultimately, to seek the care we need. By seeking to stay in negativity and dwell on it, we fall out of Jesus's will. In it, we can never go wrong.

It's important—the way we die. Don't allow desperate feelings to engulf you to the point of taking your own life. That's really what they are—just powerful feelings. I know I'm repeating myself, but you really do need to get into you that someone being suicidal is merely engulfed a set of very difficult emotions that need to be dispelled through talking and possibly medication. I know; I've been there countless times, and have countless times found relief and release from those binding feelings. Choose to let God decide when and how your life will end. Think again if you are so heavy that you're thinking about suicide. Jesus, "The one who calls you is faithful, and he will do it" (1 Thessalonians 5:24).

PSALM 77

Psalm 77 is a real working-through of deep emotions, something we need to do if we are to move forward; the psalmist takes great pains to identify and articulate his pain:

"When I was in distress, I sought the Lord; at night I stretched out untiring hands, and I would not be comforted" (verse 2b), and "I was too troubled to speak" (verse 4b). He feels "reject[ed]" (verse 7) by God. God's love has "vanished," and His promises fail (verse 8). He asks, "Has God forgotten to be merciful? Has he in anger withheld his compassion?" (verse 9).

But then the psalm takes a turn. I wonder if it does so purely because of the work the author has done to articulate and express his deep pain. The psalmist finds strength to engage faith and let it make the decision to "remember the deeds of the Lord … your miracles of long ago" (verse 11).

The psalmist works through his disillusionment and his rage, and gets to the point where he makes an active decision to dwell on good things that the Lord has done. The parting of the Red Sea is mentioned. The author also writes of the power of God displayed in a thunderstorm or an earthquake.

If you are grieving, can you identify and articulate with God, a trusted friend, counselor, or a helping group the feelings that threaten to overwhelm you? Can you find expression for these deep and troubling feelings? Can you then bring yourself to reflect on the good things God has already accomplished in your heart and life? I say again, remember this promise of God to you:

> Being confident of this, that he who began a good work in you
> will carry it on to completion until the day of Christ Jesus.
> (Philippians 1:6).

Can you believe it?

We all experience grief at one time or another, even children, such as with the death of a pet or a grandparent. With little ones feeling grief, simply model faith and trust in God, and speak with them about engaging these for themselves.

Life, Jesus says, is not easy. We will have trouble, and sometimes we can contribute to it directly ourselves. How often do we rush to do things without thinking and have an accident of some sort? Or we've failed to get enough rest or eat properly and added weight causes health problems? Or we make ourselves too busy to fit exercise into our days, and arteriosclerosis develops? Especially when we are in despair, our motivation for taking care of ourselves can dwindle, and therefore our physical health is more at risk.

We must work hard at seeking hope. Let Psalm 77 be a model for you in your pain. Express yourself thoroughly in a safe environment. Then, let faith win, not dark emotions. We can stare downward, or we can reach in and up (remember the "mud and stars" story?). We can lose heart or "take heart," as Jesus said, when we are confronted with troubles. Which will you choose?

Chapter Fifty

ON CONFINEMENT

We all go through periods of confinement, whether physically in a broken body, with a broken limb; in our minds, with mental sickness; or in our spirits, with religion that preaches salvation by works. Some individuals are incarcerated or are restricted through persecution or oppression. What an incredible sense of freedom we can experience when such periods come to an end! We can say, "I have known what it is to be confined, so I will know freedom that much more."

Sometimes the confinement does not come to a close in this lifetime. As a reminder, because of the fall in the garden of Eden by Adam and Eve, we have all been thrust into a prison of one sort or another, but rest assured that, as Christians, we will receive new bodies and live in abject bliss, once we pass from this earth: we will experience eternal freedom! In the meantime, bravely endure your confinement. "I have known what it is to be confined, so I will know freedom that much more."

SAYING NO

God gave me lessons today in saying no—no to the woman who expects me to always be there for her, no to the woman who feeds me lies, no to the man who wants to complain to me about his woes but is not willing to not work things through. "No. I cannot." Sometimes, it's hard to say it. It takes practice because sometimes we may feel fear and guilt when we say it—fear of an angry response that may lead to rejection or withdrawal of love; guilt from an unrealistic expectation that we should be an endless source of giving. The fear is not from God; if someone rejects you or withholds or withdraws his or her love from you because you said no to him or her, know that that person is not a good person for you to have in your life anyway. Let him or her back away. With regard to the guilt, it is false, for God knows none of us is an endless supply of energy and compassion. He knows the fragility of our humanness. He also knows we need to take and receive, as well as give.

Enmeshment within family members can take place as a result of boundaries that are unclear and permeable, where folks in the same family are actually too close, where the whole person is not seen, and where there is no acknowledgment of the need for personal space and identity. With enmeshment, as well as with the feeling that you could not please your caregivers from an early age, you might learn to give, over and beyond what is healthy. With such individuals, receiving good things from others, as well as from God, can be very foreign. They need to say no to their compulsions to give over abundantly out of fear of rejection and learn to give in more healthy portions from a base of love.

Maybe in our families of origin, we were trained to become doormats for others, and learning to be assertive didn't happen. If you are a victim of such abuse, don't stay a victim. Step out and be brave by getting the help you need and deserve to learn healthy boundaries, and consequently, the ability to keep yourself safe.

Learning to say no, and setting good boundaries can be very challenging at times but it is oh-so-necessary because if we cannot do so, this can lead to a heavy heart, which can lead to suicidal ideation if the situation gets out of control. Learning to say no is necessary to let God help us protect and love ourselves.

I am not Savior. Jesus is. I am human, made of flesh and bones, breakable and penetrable, fragile and frail. Jesus is the source of all power. It is He who teaches me how to care well for myself, giving me the permission and the strength to say no. Are you having trouble saying no? Seek Jesus, ask for His help, and He will supply all you need to learn to take good care of yourself and to say no when you need to.

DISPLACED FROM HOME

Many of us take having a home for granted, yet some find themselves displaced from their places of residence, either temporarily or permanently. This may be due to natural disaster or fire, but often, it's a result of aging or health problems. As a reminder, I watched as my dad's health deteriorated to such a degree that he could no longer live in his own house. In my case, I had to relinquish the apartment I had as an able-bodied person when I was living in the institution. If you have been displaced from your home, perhaps you can find comfort in these words of Jesus:

> Foxes have dens and birds have nests, but the Son of Man has no place to lay his head. (Matthew 8:20)

To know that Jesus was born in a stable, poor and unappreciated by many, and that He died the same way; to know that the majority of His life was spent roaming from place to place, without a home base, may offer some comfort to those who face letting go of the beloved place they called home.

If you have been displaced, remember that Jesus knows what you feel. Consider Him your solace, perhaps as you are forced to now call a difficult place home.

Rick Warren, in his book *The Purpose Driven Life*, has said that in order to keep us from becoming too attached to earth, God allows us to feel a significant amount of discontent and dissatisfaction in life—longings that will never be fulfilled on this side of eternity. We're not completely happy here, he says, because we're not supposed to be—earth is not our final home. We were created for something much better.

> Do not let your hearts be troubled. You believe in God; believe also in me.
>
> My Father's house has many rooms; if that were not so, would I have told you that I am going there to prepare a place for you?
>
> And if I go and prepare a place for you, I will come back and take you to be with me that you also may be where I am. (John 14:1–3)

Rest assured that God is preparing a place for you in the very home for which your soul always has been intended. Hang on to that hope as you wait in patient expectation of the coming glory in His time.

THIS LIFE A PREPARATION

Rick Warren says that this life is merely a preparation for the next. Bad things happen to good people because it is these trials that God uses to mold something beautiful, to mold spiritual riches in us. This life is transient. As a song by Casting Crowns says, we are "a wave tossed in the ocean, a vapor in the wind." What would you rather have: loads of pleasure and comfort here or spiritual riches there? After all, we are going to spend a lot more time in eternity after we die than we will spend here on earth. Do the seventy or eighty or ninety years we may live here on earth compare with eternity? God knows it doesn't. How could He be a loving God to indulge you in this life and not consider the other?

This world is said to be Satan's (John 12:31). He promotes overindulgence, obesity of body (though there may be physical reasons, not gluttony, that are involved here), mind, and spirit, lavishing with ease and pleasure. That is his domain.

God has a higher purpose. Satan is concerned with the here and now, without referring to the consequences of your decisions. God considers the sweet by-and-by.

The devil argues that a God who cares is one who spares us from troubles. God knows we need troubles as coal needs pressure for it to turn into a diamond. God is preparing for us with diamond characters to enjoy for all eternity. So hang in there! He has a purpose. We're not home yet. Let Him prepare you in the way He chooses, on His timetable.

> Though He slay me, yet will I trust Him. Even so, I will defend my own ways before Him. (Job 13:15 NKJV)

Endnotes

1   Dietrich Bonhoeffer. *The Cost of Discipleship* (New York: Simon and Schuster, 1959), 45.
2   C. S. Lewis. *The Problem of Pain* (New York: Simon and Schuster, 1996), 3.

Printed in the United States
By Bookmasters